MAKING
WELSH QUILTS

THE TEXTILE TRADITION THAT INSPIRED THE AMISH?

Mary Jenkins and Clare Claridge

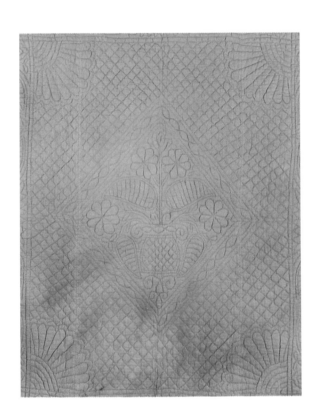

DEDICATION

To the women of Wales who made such wonderful quilts, many of whose names we do not know; we thank them for their diligence and inspiration and dedicate this book to their memory.

Text and designs © Mary Jenkins and Clare Claridge 2005
Photography and layout © David & Charles 2005

Mary Jenkins and Clare Claridge have asserted their right to be identified as authors of this work in accordance with the Copyright, Designs and Patents Act, 1988.

First published in the UK in 2005 by
David & Charles
Brunel House   Newton Abbot   Devon
www.davidandcharles.co.uk
David & Charles is a subsidiary of F+W (UK) Ltd.,
an F+W Publications Inc. company

A catalogue record for this book is available from the British Library.

ISBN 0 7153 1908 6

Paperback edition published in North America in 2005 by
KP Books, an F+W Publications Inc. company
700 East State Street, Iola, WI 54990
715-445-2214/888-457-2873
www.krause.com

A catalog record for this book is available from the Library of Congress:
2005926177

ISBN 0-89689-254-9

Printed in China by SNP Leefung

Commissioning editor   Vivienne Wells
Desk editor   Ame Verso
Art director   Ali Myer
Project editor   Katherine James
Production controller Ros Napper

Photography by Simon Whitmore, Roger Clive-Powell, Karl Adamson and Kim Sayer

PICTURE CREDITS
All images © David & Charles except: pages 7, 11, 14, 15, 102 (top right) and 103 National Museums and Galleries of Wales; page 29 Ceredigion Museum.

Frontispiece: The Brecon Star Quilt – see page 58.

Contents

INTRODUCTION

Here in Wales, quilts remind us of the homes of our parents and grandparents. We look back with nostalgia, as quilts were part of our lives then: useful, attractive but relatively unimportant and certainly not considered to be of any great value. How wrong we were! It has taken us many years to realize what treasures we have long taken for granted and to see that our quilting heritage is quite unique. We are lucky that many quilts have been saved from oblivion for us to admire and study, as a result of the foresight and dedication of a few enlightened people.

The aims of this book are to show you how Welsh quilts were made, and to inspire you to try quilting the Welsh way. We hope this will give you a greater understanding of Wales as a country, and if you can't actually travel here, that you will enjoy the quilts within these pages and even make one of your own.

THE DIFFERENT WAYS – A PERSONAL APPROACH

As you will see from the quilt projects, the authors of this book – Mary Jenkins and Clare Claridge – have very different methods of making quilts and a personal approach to selecting fabrics. You are presented with a choice: which way do you want to make your quilt? It is for you to decide.

Clare collects and lectures on Welsh quilts and has made a special study of quilting patterns; she is also known for her expertise in teaching rotary cutting. Some years ago, she began devising ways of making small-scale replicas of Welsh quilts using these techniques. Through day schools and demonstrations she has enabled many students to make a quilt very quickly and then take their time quilting it with the traditional Welsh motifs (see pages 104–112). The fabrics Clare chooses are as near as she can find to those of the original quilt, but the change in size means that the patterned fabrics may need to be smaller in scale.

Clare is a great admirer of Amish quilts and enjoys working with plain colours. Along with many other experts she has been struck by the similarity between some Amish and Welsh wool quilts, and many of her quilts reflect this fondness for simple shapes in plain and sombre colours used in a dramatic way.

Mary, on the other hand, rarely uses plain fabric. Her joy is mixing prints and she is fascinated by how one patterned fabric reacts to another. She always tries to use British fabrics in her quilts, if possible Welsh ones, and has a large collection of vintage Laura Ashley fabrics. These, together with Liberty of London fabrics, are her mainstay.

Mary's quilts are not replicas but they are made in the spirit of old Welsh quilts, usually based on the design layout of an original quilt, if not its actual colours, and using similar methods of working. As she uses small scraps of fabric, some left over from previous projects, others too small (or sometimes too precious) to use elsewhere, every piece is marked out separately. The more intricate sections are hand pieced.

Clare and Mary therefore have different ways of designing and making their quilts, which shows how Welsh quilts can appeal to quilters with different levels of expertise and experience. You may be a beginner who just needs to buy a limited amount of fabric to make something dramatic. Or you may have large amounts of fabric and be keen to try an unstructured approach – something very different, a change from working with blocks.

Opposite: The Flying Geese
Frame Quilt – see page 54.

WALES AND ITS QUILTERS

Wales is a small country with a population of around 2.75 million. Lying to the west side of the British Isles, above the Cornish peninsula, Wales shares an eastern border with central England but is otherwise surrounded by sea. The beautiful Welsh countryside, rugged coastline, hills and mountains are kept green and pleasant by a high rainfall that sweeps in from the Atlantic.

This lovely landscape is scattered with strings of castles, more than 400 of them, giving a tangible clue to its turbulent past. Democratic and political struggles over the centuries mean that Wales lost a level of aristocratic patronage long ago, and this has had a considerable effect on its heritage and culture, including its textile heritage. England, a very close neighbour, is much larger and wealthier. The English Court and Church, always patrons of the decorative arts, commissioned artists and craftspeople to decorate and adorn their palaces, cathedrals and great houses and, as they required a constant supply of high-quality items, they kept a skilled workforce busy. Unfortunately, there are few great houses in Wales. Welsh cathedrals are few in number and very modest in comparison with those in England, and many of the castles fell into ruin. So there was no demand in Wales for high-quality textiles, and little opportunity for the female population to learn fine needlework.

The upper classes in England and Wales inhabited a separate world from the rest of the population. Only they had access to the finer things in life, including fine fabrics. The lower orders, unless they were employed to serve or supply the rich, had to make do with home-spun materials and had no idea of what they were missing. There are some references in inventories of Welsh houses to bed quilts, quilted clothing and so on, and there are certainly early pieces to be seen in Welsh museums.

The earliest quilt in the collection of The Museum of Welsh Life at St Fagans is thought to date from the 18th century, and was made in Newcastle Emlyn in Ceredigion. It does display patterns that are now recognized to be Welsh in style and these patterns are thought to have been in general use at the time. Although this quilt gives us an intriguing glimpse into our quilting history, it is only one example and we do not know how typical it was of its time or how its patterns evolved.

It may seem cavalier to dismiss so many centuries of Welsh history in so few lines but in terms of early textiles, prior to the 19th century there is so little evidence it is difficult to make definitive statements about a Welsh style of embroidery or quiltmaking.

CHANGING TIMES

The Industrial Revolution at the end of the 18th century changed everything. Massive mineral deposits were discovered in Wales and great industries developed around these new resources. People flocked from all parts of Britain to work in the coal mines and in iron- and steel-making plants. Although this meant dreadful pollution of the environment and poor working conditions, people did have more money and more opportunity to buy as new markets opened up to them. They also had the chance to travel as the railways improved access to the large ports and to the ships that crossed to America and beyond. Many Welsh people travelled from the English ports of Liverpool and Bristol to North America. The new coal and steel industries there needed experienced workers, but many returned home later as there was plenty of work in Wales. There is evidence that this to-ing and fro-ing across the Atlantic had a significant effect on quiltmaking in Wales and, as we shall see later, also in the United States.

Wales changed rapidly from a poor rural economy to a highly industrialized country, especially in the south. With this came a new stature and national identity. This certainly applies to the needlework heritage. Because enormous numbers of quilts and other textiles were being made at this time it became possible to recognize a Welsh way of doing things.

THE QUILTS

The bulk of Welsh quiltmaking began in the mid-19th century and continued almost to the middle of the following century. The quilts themselves can be divided into three main categories: woollen quilts, cotton and multi-fabric quilts, and wholecloth quilts. It is this last category, the wholecloth quilts, that is most associated with Wales, probably because these were the most recent and survive in greater numbers. However, the Welsh quilt heritage is much more varied than this.

Woollen Quilts

All Welsh quilts are now much sought after, but it is the woollen quilts that have had the most dramatic reassessment of their worth. They are 'Cinderella' quilts – from being left out in the cold, literally, they have now been elevated to being hung in galleries. Until quite recently they were considered too heavy for beds and were relegated to outdoor use, many ending up covering farm vehicles or being used as horse blankets or beds for dogs.

Those made of vivid flannels are strikingly similar to American Amish quilts. Indeed, experts believe that the Amish, who had no quilt-making tradition prior to settling in America, drew their inspiration from their new neighbours, the Welsh, who had also settled in Pennsylvania. The evidence for this link between Welsh and Amish quilts is strong. Both have the same simple format, and a graphic quality that appeals to today's quilters and collectors.

Above: Teacher and students at Aberdare Technical College (1920s). The quiltmaker, Irene Morgan (née Davies), is standing on the left of the quilt. The circular centre surrounded by swirling Paisley motifs is typical of the quilts produced in the Aberdare area at that time.

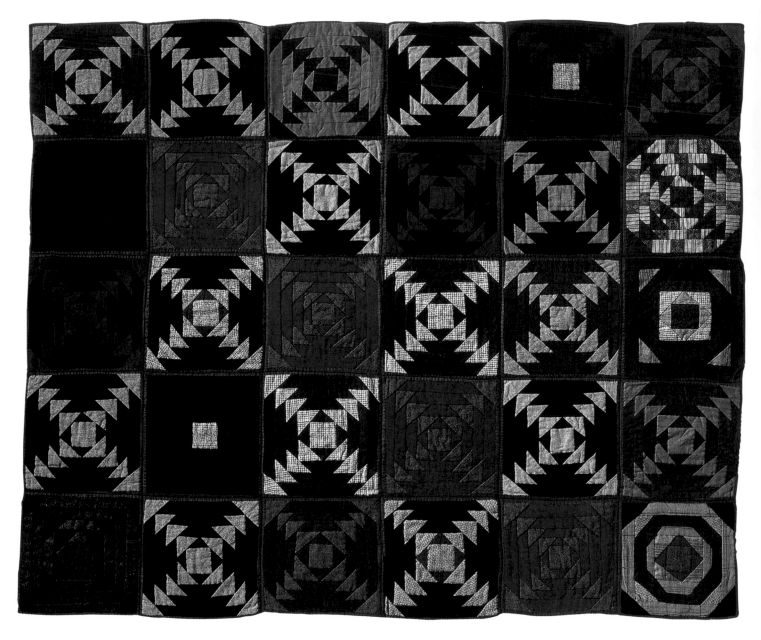

Welsh woollen quilts were made using cloth manufactured in the then thriving wool industries of mid and west Wales. The quilts were entirely home grown, made with local cloth from local sheep and filled with sheep's wool collected from the hedgerows. As a result, they were inexpensive to produce and warm to sleep under in cold, damp houses.

As many Welsh families crossed and re-crossed the Atlantic, the design influence was also two-way. This is demonstrated by the number of Welsh quilts made using American block patterns. Some were made in light fabrics as they would have been in their home country,

but the most characteristic are the block-patterned quilts made of Welsh wool. There is undoubtedly a shared quilt history between Wales and Pennsylvania and research is on-going to give a clearer picture of that time.

Cotton and Multi-Fabric Quilts

Roller-printed fabrics became generally available around 1840 and after this date cotton quilts were made in great numbers. The medallion or frame quilt is the style that is most associated with Welsh patchwork. However, in Wales patchwork was considered the poor relation. For Welsh quilters the craft was in the quilting.

Above: A Welsh wool flannel quilt, made using an American block pattern *c*.1905, 80 x 96in 203 x 243cm).
Collection of Jen Jones.

It is the quilting patterns that identify a quilt as Welsh, for the fabrics were made in the cotton mills of England.

There are many categories of quilt within this group and the fabrics used in them give many clues to the social status of the maker. This is explored in The Quilt Gallery (pages 10– 33) where specific quilts and their fabrics are discussed.

Wholecloth Quilts

From 1880, satin cotton in a range of plain colours became the favoured fabric for making quilts. The sheen on this fabric showed the patterns to perfection and must have encouraged everyone to improve their stitching.

Between the two World Wars quilting skills were given a boost by the setting up, in 1928, of the Rural Industries Board, an organization formed to encourage craft industries in areas suffering economic depression. The mining valleys of South Wales were one such area and the Board contacted all the skilled quilters it could find and asked them to recruit and train others. The object was to make high-quality quilts to sell as luxury items in wealthier areas. This raised the standard of quilting, as only the best work was accepted and quilters were encouraged to use the traditional patterns in new ways. It also created a structure within which to learn the craft and many quilting classes were formed. Competitions were held and keenly contested. Beautiful quilts were made, the ultimate goal being to receive a prize from the Eisteddfod, the annual national gathering for the promotion of Welsh arts.

During World War II production of the fabric necessary for making quilts ceased. Women's lives changed as they played their part in the war effort. When normal life eventually resumed after the war, only a few keen quilters continued with their craft and there were few new recruits. Aspirations had changed, the world had moved on and so a long era of quilting in Wales came to an end.

MORE RECENT TIMES

In the late 1960s the Laura Ashley company opened its first factory in Carno in mid-Wales in what was to be the start of a global business empire. Fortunately for quilters, Laura loved patchwork and had a collection of quilts that inspired many of her famous fabric prints. She knew that her fabrics appealed to quilters and catered to them by selling off-cuts at the factory. This was manna from heaven for quilters and bags of Laura Ashley patchwork pieces were the basis of much of the patchwork produced at that time.

In the 1970s, a revival of interest in patchwork and quilting led to the creation, in 1979, of The Quilters' Guild. Many Welsh Guild members formed groups to promote the craft and encouraged others to join them.

In those days, obtaining suitable fabrics for patchwork was a challenge and the range of wadding (batting) and other specialist supplies was limited. Of course, Welsh traditions were ignored, as it was American quilts that everyone aspired to, helped by the seemingly limitless supply of fabrics, books and magazines produced in America.

THE QUILTERS

The reason for the distinctive style and consistently high standard of quilting found on Welsh quilts is that the majority of it was professional work. This was not a social activity shared by groups of women, as in North America, but a way of earning a living. In Wales it was the custom, if you could afford it, to employ a quilter rather than undertake the task yourself. Of course, housewives did make and quilt their own patchwork but few examples have survived as homemade quilts were used and worn out. Quilts that were paid for were kept for best, treated carefully, and have lasted.

Other quilters travelled around within an area, sometimes with an apprentice, living with the customer while making the quilt. These quilters worked quickly and it is said that they could produce a quilt in two weeks – which, if you examine their intricate designs, was no mean feat.

In the 20th century, under the patronage of the Rural Industries Board, quilting did become a group effort with up to four women working on one quilt. Again, this was not for social reasons but because they were under pressure to produce high-quality work quickly.

Though these later 20th-century quilts were undoubtedly beautiful and set standards for all quilters to aspire to, they do not have the boldness and vitality of the earlier quilts. The structure and discipline of a quilting class or a cooperative meant that the personality of the quilter was inevitably suppressed. When a teacher dictated the design and demanded perfect stitching from her students there was no scope for individual input. In earlier times it was the quilter's unique style that was admired – her quilts were sought after because they bore the stamp of her personality.

THE QUILT GALLERY

O n the following pages is a collection of many different quilts made in Wales between 1820 and 1930. Some are drawn from museum and other large collections but many belong to individuals who have either inherited them or bought them because they wanted to own a piece of Welsh textile history. The aim in selecting these quilts was that they should reflect the wide range of quilts made throughout Wales at that time.

LLANDEILO CHINTZ QUILT

The quilt pictured opposite was made in Llandeilo in Carmarthenshire by Rachel Williams and belonged to Ann, the wife of William Williams, a maltster in the town. That is all the information recorded when the quilt was donated to The Museum of Welsh Life and we can only speculate about the relationship between the owner and the quilter. Although they have the same surname they need not necessarily have been related as so many people in Wales are called Williams. Indeed, researching family history in Wales is extremely difficult as so many people share a limited number of names and Williams is one of the most common. However, the quality and intricacy of the quilting suggests that Rachel Williams was a professional quilter and if it wasn't a gift to a family member, any-one commissioning such a high-quality quilt would need to have been fairly affluent to afford it.

It is a very simple medallion quilt, made with large pieces of expensive fabric, with a printed central panel surrounded by a series of borders in shades of beige, fawn and blue in printed floral cottons. The back of the quilt is unusual in that it is also of patchwork made with the same fabrics but in a much simpler form. Normally a quilt with such an elaborate quilted design would have had a plain backing in order to show the patterning to greater effect.

The quilting designs are very beautiful with a centre consisting of a large roundel quartered and filled with veined leaves and bordered with a diamond edging.

There are quarter circles at the corners of the centre field and a wonder-ful array of subsidiary patterns including ferns, leaves, hearts and spirals.

The deep inner border is filled with a bold chevron design with spiral infill. The outer border, which is now very worn, is quite narrow and again filled with a diamond pattern.

Opposite: Llandeilo Chintz Quilt
c.1800–30, 83 x 101in (207 x 253cm),
The Museum of Welsh Life, St Fagans.

PEMBROKESHIRE CHINTZ QUILT

This magnificent quilt is made with large pieces of glazed chintz in a simple format, rather like one large block. However, the fabrics are worthy of their scale and have retained their colour and freshness so that they gleam as much as they would have done when the quilt was first made.

It is one of six quilts retrieved from England where they had been taken by a member of the Morgan family, originally from Pembrokeshire. They are now back in Wales, as this quilt, with another one from the same family, is part of Jen Jones's collection and is on regular display.

It has been exhibited all over the world, always showing its patchwork side so its reverse is seldom seen. This is a great pity as the wonderful quilting is certainly worthy of display, and its intricacy adds great richness and depth to the chosen chintzes. It has very sophisticated patterning, consisting of a central urn filled with a large five-leaved plant and other flower forms set within a circle of curved leaves. There are four smaller flower-filled urns at each corner of the quilt, all set within a twisted cable border. The space surrounding the central area is filled with cross-hatching dotted with star motifs. It is truly a tour de force of quilting.

Right: Pembrokeshire Chintz Quilt, reverse (quilted) side c.1820, 72 x 82in (183 x 208cm), Collection of Jen Jones.

Above: Pembrokeshire Chintz Quilt – patchwork side. The flowery chintz and roller-printed striped fabrics of the outer border mask the wonderful quilting border design of swags filled with elaborate tulip and fan motifs (see page 12, bottom right).

NEWPORT CHINTZ QUILT

This is another large-scale patchwork quilt made in Pembrokeshire around 1830. The patchwork side is made with some lovely glazed cotton prints but its construction is extremely simple, consisting as it does of such large pieces. Thus the patchwork side pales to insignificance when you turn to the reverse and examine the quilting.

The quilter has worked a very sophisticated central design of an urn filled with flower shapes, though these flowers motifs do follow the traditional Welsh quilting form. The eight-petalled flower or rose motifs in particular are carried out into the borders, which helps to give cohesion to the overall design. This central area is cornered with four smaller flower-filled urns and areas of cross-hatching are worked around

the motifs and then carried into the corner squares of the first border.

The design content thus far is very similar to that of the Pembrokeshire Chintz Quilt (page 12) although the patterns are quite different. However, because it is so large, this quilt has space for two wonderful borders which, though carefully planned, are less sophisticated than the central area. Now we can see the Welsh quilting tradition shining through, with the large hearts in the first border and the flowing leaf shapes interspersed with tulips, eight-petalled flowers and spirals in the outer border.

The quilter has carried out highly decorative and elaborate patterning. It looks very complicated indeed but at the same time has remained true to the traditional motifs that were so widely practised by all Welsh quilters.

Below: Newport Chintz Quilt, reverse (quilted) side *c.*1830–40, 89 x 104in (224 x 260cm), The Museum of Welsh Life, St Fagans.

Above: Newport Chintz Quilt – patchwork side.

THE TAILOR'S QUILT

No book on Welsh quilts would be complete without this remarkable coverlet made between 1842 and 1852 by James Williams, a master tailor of Wrexham. It consists of 4,525 pieces of woollen cloth, mainly from military uniforms, and its colours reflect their colour range, being mainly blue, red, brown, grey and fawn.

This wonderful piece includes scenes from the Bible, representations of animals and Welsh landmarks such as the Menai suspension bridge and the Ruabon viaduct, complete with a cross-ing steam train. These are surrounded by panels of geometric patchwork and on each corner are the emblems of the four countries that form the British Isles: the leek (Wales), shamrock (Ireland), rose (England) and thistle (Scotland).

Though meticulously pieced, the Tailor's Quilt has astonishing freedom in its design and one marvels how these two elements could be combined so successfully. Although James Williams earned his living through precise tailoring work, he was undoubtedly a free spirit with a natural ability to express his creativity.

Right: Swansea
Patchwork Quilt *c*.1850,
77 x 88in (196 x 224cm),
Private collection.

SWANSEA PATCHWORK QUILT

This quilt was discovered by its present owner
in the attic of her parents' house in Swansea.
Nothing is known of its history as it lay undis-
covered for many years but its fabrics date it to
the mid-19th century.

It is quite an elaborate piece of patchwork
with 14 borders or frames and was obviously
carefully planned, which is not always the case
with Welsh patchwork.

Although parts of the quilt are quite worn
(in fact some fabrics are disintegrating) it was
obviously a cherished heirloom, as at some
time in its history it has had major restoration.
Someone has given it a new backing and added
another layer of quilting. This was probably
intended to strengthen the quilt and give it a
new lease of life, but it has made the quilting
patterns difficult to decipher. However, they are
undoubtedly Welsh in style.

THE BLACKWOOD QUILT

This dowry quilt also has elaborately planned patchwork but only eight borders. It was brought in 1885 by Fanny Haskell from Bedwellty near Blackwood in Monmouthshire to Ynysbwl near Pontypridd in Glamorganshire on her marriage to William Evans. The young couple set up home in Ynysbwl, running the Post Office and general store there until Fanny died when she was only 37. They had four children, and the quilt was passed down to Fanny's grandson John and his wife Rosemary.

However, we don't know if Fanny made this quilt herself – it could have been made for her by someone else as part of her dowry.

Although the quilt has been very intensively quilted, the quilting patterns are not in high relief. This is because the quilt has a very thin cotton filling, not a woollen filling like most of the best Welsh quilts. The charm of this quilt lies in the wonderful selection of cotton prints that have been used in the quilt's piecing, which are so typical of those found in the best frame quilts of the period.

Left: The Blackwood Quilt *c.*1880, 72 x 96in (180 x 204cm), Private collection.

GALLERY

HIRED HAND QUILT

This quilt is in the collection of the Quilt Association at the Minerva Gallery, an art centre based in Llanidloes, dedicated to the study and collection of Welsh quilts. Exhibitions of quilts and related textiles are held here regularly.

Llanidloes is an ancient market town and centre of wool production, almost in the middle of Wales at the base of the sheep-filled slopes of the Cambrian Mountains, with the rivers Severn and Clwywedog flowing nearby. It still has its Tudor Market Hall, where the fleeces were originally traded, together with terraces of old weavers' cottages.

As the name suggests, this is a utilitarian quilt made by the most rudimentary means for the use of farm hands, grooms, and similar workers. This category of staff usually lived in extremely primitive conditions and a warm quilt was necessary for their well-being. Because of their hard usage it is rare to find a quilt of this type in such good condition, which is one of the reasons for the inclusion of this example in the collection of the Quilt Association. The other reason is that the cloth from which it was made was manufactured in the mills of that area of mid-Wales.

Although these quilts were usually made up very quickly, it is clear that someone did make some effort to grade and arrange the patches on this quilt. The colours are sombre but it does have a subtle charm.

Below: Hired Hand Quilt *c.*1880, 70 x 76in (178 x 193cm), Collection of the Quilt Association, Llanidloes.

Right: Wool Flannel
Quilt *c.*1880, 72 x 74in
(183 x 188cm),
Collection of Jen Jones.

WOOL FLANNEL QUILT

This quilt from Synod Inn, Ceredigion, is dated 1880. The sombre rust
and navy woollen flannels of one side are enlivened by the addition of
four vivid red squares, while the back is a rich gold wool. Its design is
bold and very simple, but it is heavily quilted despite the double thickness of woollen fabric and a wool filling. A central square-on-point is
filled with four large leaves bordered with spirals, the surrounding areas
are filled with cross-hatching, and the outer borders are also decorated
with leaves and spirals. An unusual motif, the Welsh scissors (shown in
detail, right), is incorporated into both the centre medallion and the outer
border of the quilt.

Right: The Welsh scissors
quilting pattern on the
Wool Flannel Quilt.

WOOLLEN PINWHEEL QUILT

This is the second reversible quilt in the Gallery (see page 11), but such quilts are a comparatively rare find. On one side is a central pinwheel in red and black surrounded by simple borders of green, gold and black. The reverse is a rather haphazard arrangement of many borders interspersed with rectangles surrounding a central nine-patch block. The quilt is intensively quilted with traditional motifs of leaves and spirals, which, given the thickness of double woollen layers, was no mean feat.

Quilts like this were made with no pretensions of grandeur. They were meant to be used, so this quilt is a rare survivor.

SENNYBRIDGE QUILT

This quilt (opposite) has enormous charm, yet it has a very simple design form: a variation of the log cabin pattern. The lovely colours are still fresh and true, which probably explains why the quilt is so captivating. The fabrics used are mainly wool and heavy cotton, and the quilting is very basic indeed – just enough to hold the quilt together.

This quilt was made in Sennybridge, a village near Brecon, in the early 20th century.

Above left: Woollen
Pinwheel Quilt *c.*1850,
81 x 76in (203 x 193cm),
Collection of Jen Jones.

Left: Reverse side of the
Woollen Pinwheel Quilt.

Above: Sennybridge Quilt,
early 20th century,
72 x 76in (182 x 193cm),
Brecknock Museum
and Art Gallery.

STARFISH QUILT

This quilt perfectly encapsulates the two contrasting aspects of Welsh quilts, where simple patchwork is partnered with elaborate quilting; a philosophy shared by Welsh and Amish quilters. However, because wool was used as a filling, the quilting in Welsh quilts appears richer and more sculptured. Also, the patterns in Welsh quilts are more varied and idiosyncratic than Amish patterns.

The Starfish Quilt is from Pembrokeshire. It is made in just two colours, red and taupe, in thick woven cotton that looks almost like sailcloth. The patchwork format is very simple indeed, consisting of a square-on-point within a wide border. This square floats on its background and does not touch its enclosing border, a feature found on many Welsh quilts. This would now be considered bad design, but it does seem to work very well on this quilt.

The quilting is sumptuous and the patterns have a definite maritime theme, which is unusual. Perhaps it was a special commission and the quilter drew inspiration from her home surroundings, as in Pembrokeshire you are never far from the sea. She used very unusual starfish motifs and a striking crab's claw design, while the centre field is separated from the borders by a sturdy double cable or rope. She also used a handsome Welsh trail for the main outer border and included many traditional motifs such as the rose and spirals as infill. The centre of the quilt is composed of the crab's claws design surrounded by four elaborate urns filled with tulips, a favourite motif often used on quilts from this county.

Below: The crab claw quilting design on the Starfish Quilt.

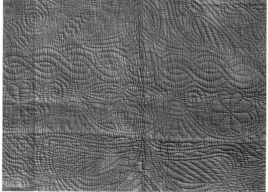

Above: Other quilting designs on the Starfish Quilt.

Above: Starfish Quilt
*c.*1880. 82 x 95in
(208 x 241cm),
Collection of the Quilt
Association, Llanidloes.

STRIPPY QUILT

The strippy quilt is a traditional form of patch-work, usually associated with the North of England but also made in Wales. Earlier 19th-century Welsh strippies were usually made in combinations of red and white, or dark blue and red woollen fabrics. By the 20th century cotton sateen was the favoured fabric in fashionable colours, such as green, pink, gold and cream. This beautiful quilt made in the 1930s in Nelson in the heart of the South Wales Valleys by Sarah Rees is typical of its time.

In 1928 the Rural Industries Board began its programme of recruiting quilters in the valleys of South Wales (see page 9). This strippy was made to the high standards set by the Board. Its traditional wool filling has been quilted in the usual Welsh way: the pattern has the central field, borders and corner pieces, and is worked across the patchwork stripes, ignoring the pieced boundaries. Occasionally a Welsh strippy is found with motifs worked within the striped areas, in the style of English North Country quilts.

Right: Strippy Quilt
*c.*1930, 72 x 80in
(183 x 203cm),
Private collection.

Right: Four Patch Quilt
*c.*1854, 82 x 90in
(208 x 229cm), Collection of Ron Simpson.

FOUR PATCH QUILT

This quilt, made with a multitude of different printed cotton fabrics, is signed and dated: 'E. Atkinson, Aged 14, 1854'. It consists of 169 four-patch blocks, set on point, combined with 144 alternating squares. Perhaps the young maker had help from an adult, as a certain degree of planning is evident. Pink triangles in just one fabric have been used to fill in around the edges of the variously patterned blocks and then a deep chintz border was added. These help to give definition and presence to this lovely scrap quilt, though it still has a delightfully un-coordinated look.

The Four Patch Quilt is backed with white cotton fabric and filled with wool. Its quilting pattern is a lattice with traditional Welsh spirals, a simple and effective choice for a young quilter. Ron Simpson, who owns the quilt, thinks that while the patchwork may have been made by the daughter of a well-to-do family who had access to interesting fabrics and enough time to make intricate blocks, it was then handed over to the sewing maid or local quilter for finishing.

BOW TIE QUILT

The Bow Tie Quilt was made in Llangurig, about five miles from Llanidloes, of locally produced wool cloth, in this case many different suiting samples. It is worked in a bow tie pattern of dark blocks alternating with blocks of red and black flannel. The red and black blocks give the design cohesion, and the dark blocks, made of many different shades of dark fabric, give a variety of tone that adds to the quilt's

overall liveliness. The combination of the two differently coloured blocks gives this quilt its dramatic impact.

There is no filling in this quilt, just a top and backing – it was obviously thought to be heavy enough without adding a woollen fleece as wadding (batting), and the quilting is simple. No attempt has been made to quilt fancy patterns; in this case the quilter has simply outline-quilted each patch.

Right: Bow Tie Quilt
c.1880, 83 x 90in
(211 x 229cm),
Collection of the Quilt
Association, Llanidloes.

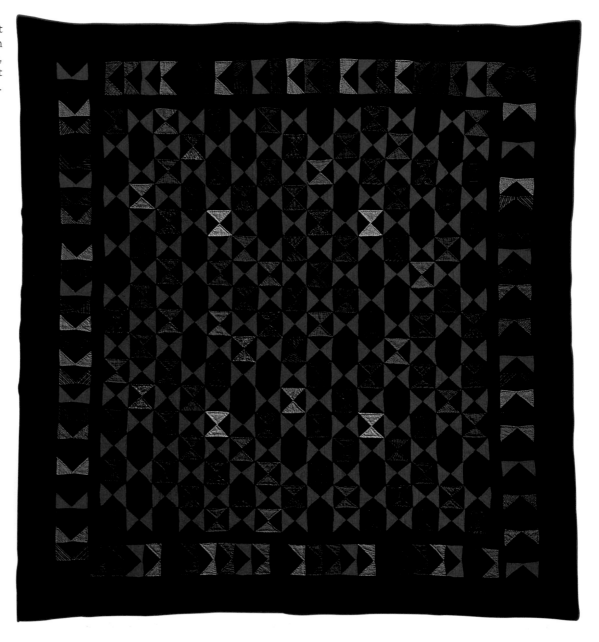

Left: Flying Geese and
Star Quilt, *c.*1870,
75 x 88in (190 x 223cm),
Collection of Jen Jones.

FLYING GEESE AND STAR QUILT

This quilt must surely have been influenced by American block patterned quilts, but what a feat of hand piecing to make it in Welsh wool. This quilt is one of a group made with similar block designs with bound edges, which were found near Llanidloes in mid-Wales. How such an elaborate pattern came to be made in a remote part of Wales is a mystery, as it is certainly not a traditional Welsh one. This quilt's only claim to Welshness lies in its locally produced Welsh wool fabric.

No attempt has been made to do elaborate quilting as the fabrics are so thick that this would be impossible. Also, when a quilt has intricate piecing, complicated quilting can distort the appearance of the patchwork pattern, especially in one such as this made of thick wool.

It also has a bound edge which was traditional on American quilts, not the butted edge which is usually found on Welsh quilts.

TWO WOOL QUILTS

These two quilts have much in common. They were made in the same area of Wales, around the same time, using similar wool fabric from the thriving local woollen industry. Yet they illustrate two very different design styles found in Welsh quilts of the latter half of the 19th century. The quilt shown below is traditionally Welsh, medallion (or frame) in form and construction; while the quilt opposite is constructed in blocks of patterns,

the favoured way of making quilts in the United States and Canada.

Very little is known of the history of these two quilts, so we can only guess why one shows such distinctive North American block-pattern construction. Perhaps a relative who had emigrated to North America sent the pattern home to Wales where it was made up in woollen fabric? Or did the quilter return home and make quilts using the method

Below: Reversible Woollen Quilt, Carmarthenshire c.1860, 77 x 87in (196 x 222cm), Private collection.

learnt across the Atlantic? We know that many immigrants did return home, but their stories are in most cases lost to us and we can only guess at the true circumstances.

Though we don't know who made these quilts, or where exactly, we do know that they are from the counties of Cardigan (Ceredigion) and Carmarthen. The block-pattern quilt is in the collection of Ceredigion Museum and is known to come from the south of that county. The medallion quilt was found in Carmarthenshire, so it is assumed to have been made there. The cloth most probably came from one of the 50 local mills then manufacturing and exporting vast amounts of woollen cloth all over the world.

REVERSIBLE WOOLLEN QUILT

Both sides of this quilt (left) are constructed in the traditional Welsh way: the medallion (or frame) form. A simple central block pattern is framed by a selection of borders (frames). The outer border is made from lengths of one fabric; the others are of pieced patchwork, made up of squares, and rectangles. All the shapes are simple because the cloth is thick and difficult to work. The fabrics used are varied: suiting samples have been alternated with bright striped and checked flannels, making the overall effect fresh and vivid.

Because of the thickness of this quilt (two woollen tops and a filling of sheep's wool), the quilting is fairly basic. There are none of the usual patterns of spirals, leaves and hearts. Regardless of this, such wool and flannel quilts are now greatly admired and sought after. Very few remain (especially in good condition), and, as wool is no longer manufactured in any quantity in Wales, it is impossible to replicate these quilts. They are probably the only tangible product left of a once important part of Welsh industrial history.

RED BASKETS, WELSH FLANNEL QUILT

This unusual and striking quilt (above) certainly has the wow factor. It is such an interesting combination of sombre suiting fabrics (commonly used in quilts of the time), with basket blocks in contrasting red flannel.

If you look closely you will see that no two blocks in this quilt are alike. They all have different combinations of suiting fabric in sombre grey, fawn, mid-blue and navy-blue – which could possibly be mill or tailors' samples. Against these muted fabrics the red baskets sing out and lift the quilt into an altogether different category. The thickness of the cloth has led to inaccuracies in the piecing of the patchwork, but it all seems to add to the charm of this quilt. There has been no attempt at fine quilting, only outline quilting and simple backing with a cotton sheet.

Above: Red Baskets, Welsh Flannel Quilt *c.*1870, 62 x 76in (155 x 190cm), Collection of Ceredigion Museum.

QUILT WITH NORWICH RIBBONS

This quilt is made of a mixture of fabric types including pieces of Paisley shawl, furnishing brocades, thick woven cottons, and silk ribbons, and it is backed with Turkey red Paisley patterned cotton. When assessed during The Quilters' Guild Heritage Project in 1990, the ribbons were identified as Norwich Ribbons – Norwich, together with Coventry, was one of the main centres of ribbon making in Britain. The stiffening process used in the manufacture of ribbons meant that they usually rotted over time, so this quilt is a rare survivor; it is in pristine condition, with the ribbons and all the other fabrics showing their original colours.

Below: Quilt with Norwich Ribbons *c.*1880, 70 x 86in (178 x 218cm), Private collection.

Although the fabrics used in the quilt are of high quality, the quilt itself is not sophisticated. Nothing is known of its history but we can speculate that it falls into a certain category of Welsh quiltmaking: the tradition in affluent households whereby the mistress of the house would select fabrics from all available sources and instruct the maids to make it into quilts. The idea was that the quiltmaking kept the maids busy in the evening (and so were less likely to 'get up to mischief') while new quilts were produced cheaply for use in the house. The fabrics in the Norwich ribbon quilt are very mixed. The quilt is very well made, but there is no attempt at fancy quilting, just a pattern of double cross-hatching over the entire quilt – not something worthy of a professional quilter but perhaps a method maids would readily choose.

However, one interesting fact weakens the above theory. It has been noted that when Turkey red Paisley patterned fabrics became popular as backing fabric for quilts, the quilting style did become simpler. Elaborate quilting designs did not show up on such dramatic fabrics so fancy patterns were not thought to be worth the effort.

PINWHEEL FRAME QUILT

The quilt opposite is the one that first inspired Clare to replicate Welsh quilts using rotary cutting methods, and the instructions and quilting patterns for making your own version are on pages 80–85. The original quilt, dated around 1880, is now in the collection of The Quilters' Guild of the British Isles. Prior to this it belonged to Ron Simpson, a well-known dealer and collector, and was regularly exhibited as part of his touring collection, but little is known of its history.

The Pinwheel Frame Quilt has a simple but striking design and is made of woollen fabrics in cream, brown and turquoise blue, together

with the remains of a Paisley shawl. The particular shade of petrel blue woollen fabric seen here, together with a similar-weight fabric in red, were often used to make petticoats. These brightly coloured undergarments were worn beneath the overdress (betgwn), which was in a more sombre hue, such as black, dark blue or grey; the overdress was caught back to show the petticoat.

The quilting patterns are not worked according to the methods normally found on Welsh quilts, where it was usual for the patterns to be worked across the boundaries of the patchwork. In this quilt the patchwork areas have first been outline quilted and then patterns have been worked within each patchwork piece. However, the motifs do follow Welsh traditions, consisting of spirals, fans and waves.

Above: Pinwheel Frame Quilt c.1880, 77 x 84in (193 x 210cm), Collection of the Quilters' Guild of the British Isles.

FOUR RED AND WHITE QUILTS

Red and white has always been a favourite colour combination with quilters, and nowhere more so than in Wales. Throughout the second half of the 19th century and up until World War I, red and white quilts like the ones shown here were made usually in cotton fabric, by Welsh quilters. Perhaps because of the impracticability of the white fabric they were generally kept for 'best', and according to some were the preferred 'wedding' quilt. Many were traditional strippies or simple geometrics like the checkerboard opposite, which actually reverses to a strippy. Others, like the two red, green and white quilts shown here, were appliqué and could be mistaken for American quilts if it were not for the quilting patterns. Many Welsh men emigrated to America during the late 19th century to work in the coal and steel industries and the women in their families were obviously influenced by the quilts they saw there. Some were sent home as presents or returned with their makers.

Mary Samuels of Aberdare went to Scranton, Ohio with her husband William, shortly after getting married, but returned home to Wales in 1891 for the birth of their daughter, Blodwen. The design of the quilt that she made for her daughter, which is seen below, shows that she had been strongly influenced by American appliqué quilts. However, it is heavily quilted in an entirely Welsh way. There is a central diamond medallion with a pot containing flowers and leaves, two borders with large fans in the corners, and leaves, spirals and roses as infill.

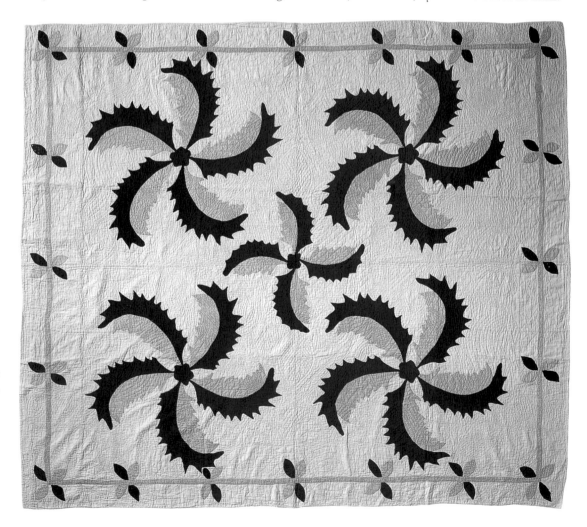

Right: Blodwen's quilt c.1891, 86 x 76in (218 x 193cm), is made from Turkey red and green cotton applied to a white calico background, in a swirling design known as 'Princess of Wales' feathers'. Private collection.

Above: A late 19th-century Welsh quilt made in Carmarthenshire *c*.1910, 90 x 80in (228 x 203cm) – a real bobby-dazzler with its zany sawtooth border and central quilted wheel-like medallion. Author's collection.

Above: The third cotton quilt belonging to this family is a red, white and gold 'Irish chain' from the early 1900s, 79 x 67in (200 x 170cm). It is of uncertain origin, stitched by machine and barely quilted at all. Private collection.

Right: A second appliqué quilt *c*.1890 80 x 75in (203 x 190cm), owned by Mary Samu-el's family has a mixed pedigree, consisting of nine appliqué blocks each quilted separately, but using traditional Welsh motifs. Private collection.

CHOOSING FABRIC

The majority of 19th-century Welsh cotton and multi-fabric quilts were unsophisticated, with little planning. They contained almost every type of printed fabric imaginable, though most of these fabrics were not made specifically for patchwork. Selling mill samples for patchwork was an offshoot of the clothing and domestic fabric market. The situation today is very different, with a multi-million-dollar international fabric industry, making and selling fabric specifically for patchwork.

FABRIC IN OLD QUILTS

As can be seen in the old quilts in this book, the quality and type of fabrics used in Welsh quilts varied greatly, ranging from woollen material to expensive chintz and mass-produced printed cottons. Only the wool quilts were made of fabric actually manufactured in Wales; all other quilts were made with materials available throughout Britain.

The home-produced wool quilts varied considerably in density and design because the individual mills manufactured cloth for specific uses, so that quilts made of off-cuts from a certain mill took on a distinctive look.

The basic format of many of the most expensively produced cotton quilts might simply have been to show off their sumptuous fabrics. The more affluent who could afford costly fabric did not really want to cut it up into small pieces. It was far more practical to use larger pieces to form the patchwork and then pay a professional to work quilting on the reverse. This close quilting with its intricate patterning and distinctive motifs added extra depth and richness of texture to these already lovely prints, making extremely beautiful and unique quilts.

Of course, the poor couldn't work this way. They had to use what they had to hand or what they could buy cheaply, so their quilts were not always so decorative. However, there are many quilts that fall between these rich and poor categories, which are made from mixed fabrics reflecting the dress and furnishing fashion of the times.

Welsh cotton and multi-fabric quilts, in common with those made in the rest of Britain, displayed every type of fabric manufactured during the 19th century. There are many quirky fabrics to be found in 19th-century quilts, and some of these look surprisingly modern. Certain categories of fabrics were always present: stripes and checks because they were manufactured for everyday clothes, Paisleys and tartans because they were fashion constants throughout the Victorian era.

Top: Quilt made of striped woollen fabric which was traditionally used for making petticoats. Middle: A variety of different fabrics were used in this quilt including silk ribbons, pieces of Paisley shawl and upholstery remnants. Bottom: A simple quilt made in Llangwm, Pembrokeshire. It was common practice to use a bright cotton handkerchief as a central panel and surround it with fabric samples bought in swatches.
Opposite: Swatches like these were sold in 19th-century drapers' shops and used to make basic patchwork.

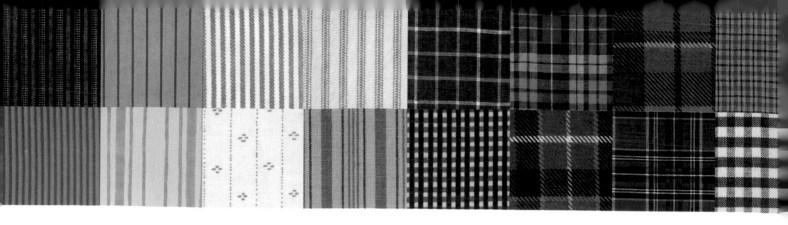

Top left: Striped fabrics of varying widths and tones.
Top right: Small and medium-scale tartan and check fabrics.
Bottom left: Small geometric prints.
Bottom right: Small multicoloured flower prints.

A DIFFERENT APPROACH

Today's quilters are used to planning their projects, measuring and co-ordinating their fabrics, and cutting into lengths of fabric rather than using scraps. Within today's teaching structure, with its emphasis on block patterns and quick techniques, it is difficult for modern quilters to work in the unco-ordinated way of traditional Welsh quilters. This would mean unlearning all the rules, and abandoning the normal design processes and methods.

How to Begin

Because it is impossible for today's quilters to think themselves back in time, we have devised a method of working that combines organization with improvization. We want our new Welsh quilts to look attractive in an unplanned way but we do need some rules to follow. So where do you start?

As everyone has a favourite range of colours, why not keep to that? If you are trying a new way of working, at least use what you are comfortable with. You probably have a very wide range of fabrics in the colours that you like best and this is a great advantage. Old Welsh quilts usually contained lots of different prints and you really do need a wide variety of similar colours and patterns of fabric to achieve the same effect.

Of course one golden rule does still apply. Always include a mixture of light, medium and dark fabrics in every piece you make. All the best patchwork has this, even Welsh quilts, despite their haphazard planning. The makers of the best Welsh quilts did this instinctively.

Quilters often overlook light and dark fabrics when forming a collection, which is why we sometimes end up with a collection of fabric in medium tones. Make a special point of building up a varied collection of such fabrics. No matter what colour range you use, you will need them.

Do not over co-ordinate: although we have all been taught to strive for a balanced look, only go part way. Carry colours through, but do it with several fabrics of the same colour, not just one. When you have a row of light and dark fabrics, use different lights and darks, and vary their tone.

Talking You Through

If you want to put these ideas into practice, choose one of the project quilts and try a different colour scheme to the one suggested. Use it as an experiment in fabric selection. Choose a keynote fabric (multi-coloured, suggesting an overall colour scheme) then add other fabrics that match, contrast and generally enhance it. Try to choose fabrics of varying scale and type in a mixture of light, medium and dark tones.

The unique charm of Welsh quilts is that decisions were taken as the work progressed. Many fabrics were used and, if a quilter ran out of one fabric, she just used the next best thing.

Once you have selected your fabrics, review your choices and, if you feel the selection needs a lift, add an accent colour. For this you might need to try out lots of fabrics until you find something that gives the whole selection some zing. Some good accent colours are: yellow ochre, bright pink, purple, red, or acid green. If you do not have any of these in your collection visit your nearest fabric shop, or, as you won't need large amounts of these accent fabrics, you could ask friends if they have anything suitable.

Fabric selection is the most important and exciting part of the whole quilting process and is worth taking time over. Don't rush it. When you get stuck, walk away and have another go later. When you are satisfied with your selection, start cutting out all the pieces for the quilt, following the project instructions. Begin with the centre pieces and work outwards, pinning your pieces onto a design wall if you have one, or onto a large piece of plain fabric that you can hang or pin up. Working this way, you can cut out the whole quilt, making changes until you are happy with the final effect. Then the hard work is over, and it is just a matter of sewing everything together and quilting it!

Where to Buy Fabric

Many quilt shops hold large stocks of fabric produced specifically for patchwork. If you can't get to a shop, many have mail-order facilities and websites – online shopping is an easy way to buy a wide selection of fabrics. If you are a beginner and have not yet built up a fabric collection, you could start by buying a selection of fat quarters from one of these sources using the fabric selection guidelines in the projects.

If you already have lots of fabric, making Welsh quilts is the ideal way of using up small pieces left over from other projects, or even precious pieces that you have been saving. By using oddments you are following in the footsteps of 19th-century Welsh quilters.

You could try building up a fabric collection from other sources. Mary makes her quilts from curtaining, shirting and clothing fabrics, which she buys mostly in sales or from charity shops. She seeks out mill outlets and antique textile dealers, and occasionally obtains vintage fabric on the Internet from websites such as Ebay. Over the years she has built up an eclectic collection but is always on the lookout for more.

Collecting fabric is a way of life; using it is a bonus. Finding something a little bit different to add to your collection from an unexpected place gives an inordinate amount of pleasure, especially if it's high quality and a bargain!

Top left: Medium-scale flower prints.
Top right: Small-scale prints of scattered flowers.
Bottom left: Two-coloured flower prints.
Bottom centre: Medium and small-scale Paisley prints.
Bottom right: Large-scale flower prints.

MAKING YOUR OWN WELSH QUILTS

The following ten Welsh quilts are designed for you to make. They are grouped together according to the methods used in their making and in order of complexity. When you study them you will see that the patchwork piecing is simple, just variations on a theme. The individual styles of the quilts are achieved entirely with the fabrics chosen and the intricate quilting patterns that give them their richness of texture. One important point to note: on all old Welsh quilts the original finishing would have been a butted edge (see page 117), not a bound one as was common on Amish and other American quilts.

The first group – Mary's quilts – are made in the old way, each piece being marked out by hand and then the pieces sewn together either by hand or machine – very much as they were made in the past. They suit all levels of ability; the only difference is in size and how much time you are prepared to invest in the quilting.

These five projects are followed by Clare's designs using modern rotary-cutting techniques and machine piecing. They are arranged from the simplest to the most complex. For example, Cariad Quilt II on pages 64–67 and Pennsylvania Echo on pages 68–73 are both suitable for beginners but the Pembrokeshire Quilt on pages 86–91 requires some experience in rotary cutting.

If you would like to try both methods you could treat the Cariad Quilts I and II (pages 40–43 and 64–67) as samplers. This particular design is the only one made by both Mary and Clare, using their favourite methods and individual fabric choices, and they do look very different. As these are very small quilts you could make them both to see which method of piecing you prefer before embarking on one of the bigger projects.

Templates for the hand-pieced projects are given on pages 96–99. Quilting plans are included at the end of the individual project instructions or are on pages 92–95. Diagrams showing how to draft the most common quilting designs are given in the Welsh Quilting Patterns section, pages 104–112.

The patchwork layouts for the first five quilt projects (pages 40–63) include grid lines. These are there to guide you as you work. However, if you want to make a larger quilt, simply increase the measurement of each grid square on the layout. For example, one square of the grid can be 1, 1½, 2in (2.5, 4, 5cm) or more depending on the size required. By enlarging in this way you keep the correct proportions of the design which is based on the simple format of traditional Welsh quilts. Note, however, that this method of enlargement will not work for the rotary-cut projects (pages 64–91) because the measurements for these include seam allowances.

CARIAD QUILT I

Mary and Clare both made a doll's quilt based on an original full-sized wool quilt from Pembrokeshire. Clare's version on pages 64–67 is made in the original colours of black and red, but Mary made hers in printed fabrics and added an extra border, top and bottom, to make it rectangular to fit her doll's cot.

She chose a bright-pink striped fabric for the central heart and appliquéd it on to a black Liberty lawn scattered with bunches of white flowers. These were set against a light flower print to form the central section. Another black print was chosen and combined with an off-white flower print for the four corner blocks. The other fabrics were a small-scale black-and-white check, border prints in pink and lilac, and a purple-and-black Paisley for the border.

Apart from the black-and-white check, which was bought in Salzburg, all the other fabrics are from Laura Ashley and Liberty of London.

Cariad is the Welsh word for 'sweetheart', and the quilting design reflects this. Mary has used the heart motif to echo the theme in her hand quilting, and it is also very appropriate because this little quilt was made for a favourite doll.

The heart was a popular motif on old Welsh quilts and not just on wedding quilts, as it is both beautiful and practical, which may explain its popularity. It can be used as a central element, but it is also very useful as a filler because it is such an adaptable shape: its curves can easily be changed to fit into an odd corner.

Right: A vintage Laura Ashley china doll is comfortably tucked up under the Cariad Quilt I in Mary's childhood doll's cot, which has been dressed in antique crochet and lace. Although the doll's dress cannot be seen here, this little quilt was created to match her outfit, which is made in mauve Laura Ashley lawn.

PROJECT CARIAD QUILT I

REQUIREMENTS

This quilt is so small that it can be made with oddments of fabric following the traditional way of making doll quilts out of scraps.

▢ ½yd (0.5m) dark print for the border

▢ Selection of cotton print fabric scraps, eg bright-pink, two black with white flowers, two off-white flower prints, small-scale black-and-white check, two border prints in pink and mauve

▢ 21 x 24in (53.5 x 61cm) light cotton backing fabric

▢ 21 x 24in (53.5 x 61cm) cotton, polyester or wool wadding (batting)

▢ Sewing thread to tone with fabrics

▢ Quilting thread to tone with fabrics

> THIS QUILT WAS DESIGNED USING INCHES, SO THE METRIC MEASUREMENTS GIVEN HERE ARE APPROXIMATE.

INSTRUCTIONS

1. Copy the templates □A, △B, □E and □J on page 96–99. Mark the grain lines and label carefully.

2. Select fabrics and paste a small scrap of each in the appropriate position on a copy of Fig 1, for easy reference.

3. Trace around the templates on the reverse side of the fabrics, adding ¼in (6mm) seam allowance before cutting out.

4. Cut the strips of fabrics for the borders that do not have templates – marked A, B and C on Fig 1.

> ## TIP
>
> *Many fabrics have a reverse side which can also be used to give a slightly different tone or colourway. The Paisley border fabric in this little quilt is actually the reverse of a purple Liberty Tana lawn. Mary chose this side because it was darker and gave the quilt a more antique look.*

FINISHED SIZE: **18 x 21IN (46 x 53.5CM)**

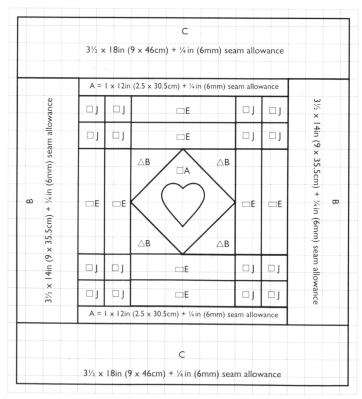

Fig 1. Patchwork layout. 1 square = 1 sq inch

Centre Medallion

1. Sew the 4 △B triangles to the centre □A square-on-point (Fig 2).

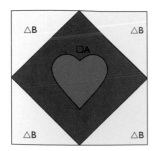

Fig 2.

2. Trace the heart template given on page 97 on to freezer paper. Cut out and press to wrong side of the fabric chosen for the heart.
3. Appliqué the heart to the centre of the square-on-point by hand, as described on page 117.

First Border

1. Join each of the 4 dark □E rectangles to a light □E rectangle (Fig 3i).

Fig 3i.

Fig 3ii.

2. Sew one of these borders on either side of the centre medallion, making sure that the dark fabric is next to the centre.
3. Join the 8 dark □J squares to a light □J square and then join these units in pairs to form 4 corner blocks, arranging them so that the dark and light squares alternate.
4. Sew a corner block to each end of the remaining 2 border sections so that the light squares are next to the dark strips (Fig 3ii).
5. Add these border units to the top and bottom edges of the central medallion (Fig 4).

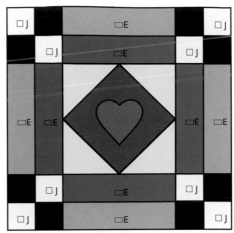

Fig 4. Joining the first border

Second (Half) Border

Cut 2 strips (A on Fig 1), each 1 x 12in (2.5 x 30.5cm) plus seam allowances, and join to the top and bottom edges of the quilt centre (Fig 5).

Fig 5.

Third (Outer) Border

1. Sew a strip (B on Fig 1), 3½ x 14in (9 x 33.5cm) plus seam allowances to either side of the quilt.
2. Finally sew a strip (C on Fig 1), 3½ x 18in (9 x 46cm) plus seam allowances to the top and bottom edges to complete the quilt top.

Quilting and Finishing

1. Cut a piece of wadding (batting) and a piece of backing fabric each 21 x 24in (53.5 x 61cm).
2. Press the quilt top carefully on the wrong side, making sure the seam allowances lie flat.
3. Layer the quilt as instructed on page 115.
4. Using the quilting plan on page 92, mark out the quilting patterns on the quilt top, as instructed on page 115.
5. Alternatively plan your own quilting designs using ideas from pages 104–112.
6. Quilt by hand following the instructions on page 116.
7. Finish the edges in the traditional butted manner (see page 117).

SUMMER QUILT

This hand and machine pieced quilt, designed and made by Mary, is one of the simplest of the traditionally pieced projects. Its medallion format is typical of old Welsh quilts: a central block surrounded by frames comprising pieced borders of squares, triangles and rectangles, or lengths of un-pieced fabric. The pink, blue and other fresh, light, colours make it a suitable gift for a baby but, as it is intensively quilted (many hours' work), this quilt is perhaps one to cherish as an heirloom.

The blue-and-pink, rose-strewn, vintage Laura Ashley fabric used in the centre of the Summer Quilt provided the initial inspiration and Mary's keynote fabric. The other fabrics were chosen to echo or contrast with the first: a mixture of light, medium and dark toned fabrics, combined with patterned fabrics of different types and scales to give a pleasing balance. In this quilt she has used self-coloured stripes, grey-and-white ticking, small flowery prints in blue, pink and pale green, and a delicate blue-and-white Toile de Jouy, which introduces a large scale without being overwhelming. The dark-green large-scaled print in the corner squares and the pale-blue and cream border print give definition to the central panel. The quilt is bordered with a dark-blue and white print.

When working your own quilt, begin by choosing a keynote fabric and then select fabrics that enhance it, following Mary's method of working (see pages 36–37) and the fabric requirements list overleaf.

The quilting design is an important factor in giving the Summer Quilt its Welsh character. The simple but traditional arrangement of patterns incorporates favourite motifs of leaves, fans and spirals, surrounded by a wave border.

You could follow Mary's suggestions or why not choose your own motifs using ideas from pages 104–112.

To show how the same layout can be used with different colour schemes, Mary has made a second quilt in a darker, richer colour palette (left). A darker version of the Laura Ashley print is combined with a rich-yellow and dark-pink Toile de Jouy, and a tartan fabric. There is a greater variety of scraps in the two (half) borders of squares-on-point (see third border), and additional corner squares, which use the tartan fabric, on the final border.

Right: Mary's alternative colourway of this quilt uses a darker, richer palette, with a greater variety of scrap-fabrics and additional corner squares.

Opposite: Summer Quilt – simple traditional piecing with intensive Welsh quilting.

PROJECT SUMMER QUILT

REQUIREMENTS

- ½yd (0.5m) blue-and-white Toile de Jouy
- ¾yd (0.75m) dark-blue fabric for borders
- Selection of fabric scraps as described on page 44, eg:
  - keynote fabric in blue and pink, possibly vintage, with roses
  - various striped fabrics in blue, pink, green and grey-and-white
  - various small-scale flowery prints in pink, blue, pale green and other light colours
  - medium-scale navy-and-white print
  - large-scale print in dark green
  - large-scale print in pale blue and cream
- 34 x 42in (87 x 107cm) light cotton backing fabric
- 34 x 42in (87 x 107cm) cotton, wool or polyester wadding (batting)
- Sewing thread to tone with fabrics
- Quilting thread to tone or contrast with fabrics

THIS QUILT WAS DESIGNED USING INCHES, SO THE METRIC MEASUREMENTS GIVEN HERE ARE APPROXIMATE.

INSTRUCTIONS

Copy the following templates on pages 96–99: □A, △B, □H, □C, □A, □G, □C, △G, □D. Mark the grain lines and label carefully. Pieces Q, L and M are simple strips of fabric, so do not need templates, but ¼in (6mm) or ½in (12mm) seam allowances should be added to the measurements given. A ½in (12mm) seam allowance is recommended for the outside edges of the border as this will give more substance to the quilted edging.

Use the patchwork layout (Fig 1, right) as a guide to cutting your fabric pieces (see page 114 for general instructions on cutting fabric pieces). You might find it helpful to cut out the pieces for the centre medallion, first, second and third borders and then to pin them to a design board. You can then stitch them a section at a time, by hand or machine (see page 115 for sewing instructions). Remember to add ¼in (6mm) seam allowance to all templates and to those pieces cut without templates.

FINISHED SIZE: **30 x 38IN (76 x 96.5CM)**

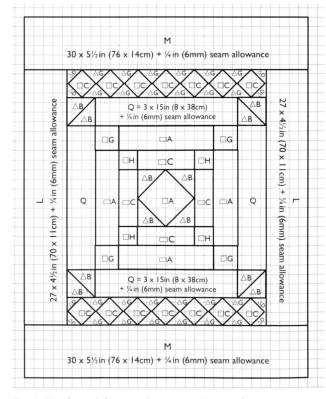

Fig 1. Patchwork layout. 1 square = 1 sq inch

Centre Medallion

1. Sew 4 △B triangles to the □A square-on-point (in keynote fabric) to form the central square.
2. Join □C rectangles to left and right sides of this square.
3. Join 1 □H square to each end of 2 □C rectangles. Join these to the top and bottom edges to complete the centre medallion.

First Border

1. Sew 1 □A rectangle to each side of the central medallion.
2. Join 1 □G square to each end of 2 more □A rectangles and sew to the top and bottom edges, as shown in Fig 2.

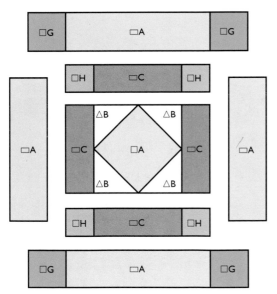

Fig 2.

Second Border

1. Cut 4 long strips (Q on Fig 1), each 3 x 15in (8 x 38cm) plus seam allowances in blue-and-white Toile de Jouy. Join a Q strip to the left and right sides.
2. Join △B triangles in pairs to form square corner units, then sew these to each end of the remaining Q strips. Make sure that the triangles are orientated correctly (see Fig 1). Attach to top and bottom edges.

Third Border

1. For this border, cut half of the △G triangles (12) and half of the △D triangles (4) in blue-and-white Toile de Jouy. Sew 1 △G and 2 △D triangles to a □C square-on-point (Fig 3i). Make 4 of these corner units, 2 reversed.
2. Sew 2 △G triangles to each of 5 □C squares-on-point (Fig 3ii). Sew these together and add a corner unit at each end to make a half border of squares-on-point (Fig 3iii). Repeat to make a second half border.
3. Attach these borders to the top and bottom edges.

Fig 3i.   Fig 3ii.

Fig 3iii.

Fourth (Final) Border

1. Cut 2 strips (L on Fig 1), each 27 x 4½in (70 x 11cm) plus seam allowances, in dark-blue border fabric. Sew an L strip to each side of the quilt top.
2. Cut 2 strips (M on Fig 1), each 30 x 5½in (76 x 14cm) plus seam allowances, in dark-blue border fabric. Sew an M strip to the top and bottom edges to complete the piecing of the quilt top.

TIP

When cutting the outer border strips, increase the seam allowance on the outer edge by an extra ¼in (6mm), in order to give a little more fabric to play with when finishing the butted edges.

Quilting and Finishing

1. Press the finished pieced top. Assemble the quilt sandwich following the general instructions on page 115.
2. Mark out the quilting design following the quilting plan on page 93, or select your own combination of patterns from the design ideas on pages 104–112). Complete the quilting by following the instructions on page 116.
3. Finish the quilt by trimming and butting the edges, see page 117.

PAISLEY STAR QUILT

The Paisley Star Quilt was made by Mary using both machine- and hand-piecing techniques. Paisley patterned fabrics were firm fashion favourites throughout the whole of the 19th century. After they became worn or damaged, many Paisley shawls were cut up and used for patchwork. In Wales the Paisley motif itself was a widely used and adapted quilting pattern (see page 105 for more information about the history of the Paisley motif in Welsh quilting patterns).

Mary designed this quilt to celebrate the enduring popularity of Paisley, and her use of the Paisley fabric immediately gives this quilt a distinctive antique look. Intensive quilting gives an extra dimension to the quilt by adding texture and strengthening the impact of its rich harvest colouring. For the quilting pattern, Mary has chosen a mixture of leaves, tulips, fans and spirals, with the Paisley motif in the border to continue the Paisley theme throughout the quilt.

Choosing Fabrics

Mary chose a large-scale woollen dress fabric as the keynote fabric for this quilt. Apart from the border, the other pieces are scraps of chintzes, stripes and geometrics in various scales, together with floral prints in mellow colours. Though she has used a variety of colours and patterns in her selection, it is the lovely yellow-ochre French chintz that gives the combination an extra sparkle. For more on Mary's method of working, see pages 34–37, which will give you more detailed help with your fabric choices. Mary has also made a variation of this quilt in a Christmas colourway (below left), showing how this quilt's layout can be used to make a quilt with other colours and types of fabric for a very different look.

If you want to make a similar quilt, choose a large-scaled Paisley fabric as your keynote fabric. Pick out the colours in the Paisley pattern and select fabrics in those colours, remembering the golden rule that you need light, medium and dark fabrics, if possible in different scales. This will not only make your quilt more interesting but will also give it an authentic Welsh look.

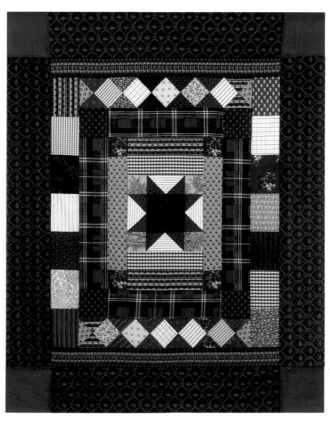

Right: This alternative Paisley Star quilt was made using a very different selection of coloured fabrics.

Opposite: The Paisley Star Quilt, using Paisley fabrics to give an antique look, and Paisley motifs in the quilting for a traditional Welsh flavour.

PROJECT PAISLEY STAR QUILT

REQUIREMENTS

- 15 × 15in (38 × 38cm) Paisley fabric
- 22 × 34in (56 × 86.5cm) border fabric
- Oddments picking out the colours of the Paisley fabric
- 35 × 42in (89 × 106cm) light cotton backing fabric
- 35 × 42in (89 × 106cm) cotton, polyester or wool wadding (batting)
- Sewing thread to tone with fabrics
- Quilting thread to tone or contrast with fabrics

THIS QUILT WAS DESIGNED USING INCHES, SO THE METRIC MEASUREMENTS GIVEN HERE ARE APPROXIMATE.

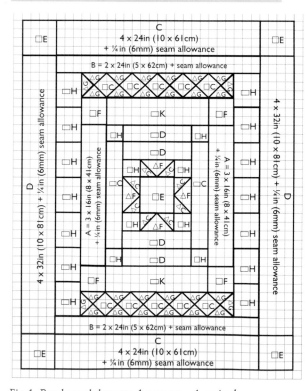

Fig 1. Patchwork layout. 1 square = 1 sq inch

TIP

Border prints were used extensively on old quilts so it's worth seeking them out to get the same effect. Buying curtaining is an economical way of obtaining longer lengths but you can buy sample pieces for the smaller areas within the quilt.

INSTRUCTIONS

1. Copy the following templates from pages 96–99: squares □E, □H and □F; triangles △C, △F and △G; rectangles □D, □C, □H and □K. Label templates for easy identification. On the wrong side of your chosen fabric, draw around the templates to mark the sewing line. Remember to add ¼in (6mm) seam allowance to each piece when cutting out.

2. You will also need the long strips of fabric marked A, B, C and D on Fig 1.

FINISHED SIZE: 32 × 40IN (81 × 102CM)

Centre Medallion

1. Sew the long edge of a △C triangle to each short side of a △F triangle, to make 4 rectangles (Fig 2).

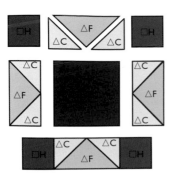

Fig 2.

2. Sew 2 of these rectangles to either side of □E square, arranging them so that the point of △F triangle faces inwards.
3. Add an □H square to either end of the remaining 2 units from step 1 and then sew them to the centre, to make the 'Star' (Fig 3).
4. Sew 1 □D rectangle to the top and bottom of the 'Star' to complete the centre medallion (Fig 4).

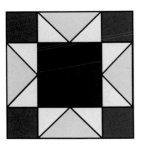

Fig 3.

Fig 4.

First Border

1. Now sew 2 □C x 2 rectangles to either side of the centre. Where a rectangular template is labelled 'x 2', this means that the strip should be cut to twice the length of the template. That is, the short side of the template is placed on the fold of the fabric.
2. Sew 2 □H squares to either end of the 2 □D rectangles and sew these to the top and bottom edges to complete the first border.

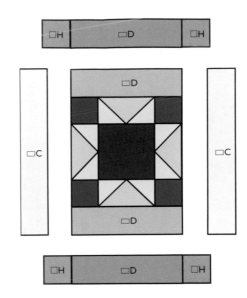

Fig 5. Assembling the first border

Second Border

1. From your Paisley fabric cut 2 □K rectangles and 2 strips (A on Fig 1), each 3 x 16in (8 x 41cm) plus seam allowances.
2. Cut 4 □F squares of dark fabric.
3. Assemble the border as shown in Fig 6.

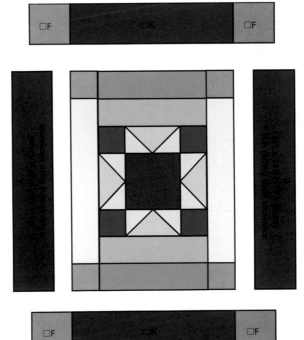

Fig 6.

PROJECT PAISLEY STAR QUILT

Third (Half) Border – Squares-on-Point

1. From an assortment of coloured scraps cut:
   - 10 light □C squares
   - 24 medium and dark △G triangles
   - 4 light △G triangles

   Arrange the triangles and squares-on-point on a flat surface, or on your design wall if you have one, using the photograph on page 50 to guide you. Pick up and sew unit by unit as follows:

2. Sew 2 medium or dark △G triangles to each □C square and sew these together in 2 rows of 5 each.

3. Sew remaining 8 △G triangles together in pairs and sew to the ends of each row (Fig 7).

4. Sew these rows to the top and bottom of the centre.

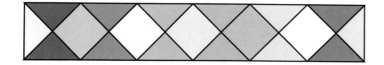

Fig 7.

Fourth Border

1. Cut 14 □H rectangles in assorted colours. Cut 2 strips of light border print (B on Fig 1), each 2 x 24in (5 x 62cm) plus seam allowances.

2. Join the □H rectangles together in 2 sets of 7 each and stitch these strips to either side of the quilt.

3. Add the long narrow strips (B on Fig 1) to the top and bottom edges.

TIP

When cutting the outer border strips, increase the seam allowance on the outer edge by an extra ¼in (6mm), in order to give a little more fabric to play with when finishing the butted edges.

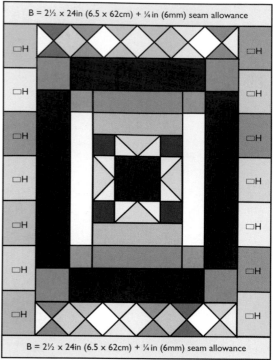

B = 2½ x 24in (6.5 x 62cm) + ¼in (6mm) seam allowance

B = 2½ x 24in (6.5 x 62cm) + ¼in (6mm) seam allowance

Fig 8. Assembling the fourth border

Final Border

1. Cut 2 strips (C on Fig 1), each 4 x 24in (10 x 61cm) plus seam allowances.
   Cut 2 strips (D on Fig 1), each 4 x 32in (10 x 81cm) plus seam allowances.
   Cut 4 □E corner squares.

2. Sew these pieces on as for First and Second Borders.

3. Press the finished top carefully.

Quilting and Finishing

1. Layer the quilt top as described in the general instructions, page 115.

2. Mark out the quilting design following the quilting plan opposite, or use a selection of your own designs from the Welsh Quilting Patterns section, pages 104–112.

3. Complete the quilting following the instructions on page 116.

4. Finish the edge in the traditional butted manner – see page 117.

Above: Quilting plan: this shows one-quarter of the whole quilt area, plus the central area of the quilting design for this project. Any spaces can be filled with extra lines and, of course, there would be a double line of quilting around the edge. The Paisley theme has been carried through to the quilting design by using the Paisley pear motif as a border pattern. All the other motifs – fans, arches, spirals – are traditionally found on old Welsh quilts. The red lines indicate the patchwork seams with the dashed red lines showing the centre lines.

Making Your Own Welsh Quilts **53**

PROJECT

FLYING GEESE FRAME QUILT

Apart from the four flying geese borders, which Mary pieced by hand, the rest of this quilt is made from very simple pieces and was sewn on the machine.

Mary has again used Paisley fabric, such a popular fabric in Welsh quilts. She actually owns curtains in this Laura Ashley fabric (pieces of which appear in this quilt), bought because it reminded her of a rather faded shawl owned by her grandmother. However, the keynote fabric is not the Paisley but the lovely vintage rose-strewn green, gold and pink Laura Ashley dress fabric; another colourway of this fabric is used in the Summer Quilt (page 44).

Choosing Fabrics

Again, like the Paisley Star Quilt (page 48), apart from the large piece of Paisley and the border fabric, this quilt is made up of scraps. There are 5 different dark greens, 10 in a medium range of soft-red/orange/pink/brown, and 12 different light fabrics of varying density. The gold-and-red Toile de Jouy was added as an accent colour. Tips on how to mix scraps are given on pages 34–37.

Today dress-weight fabrics are the recommended norm but if you study old quilts you will see that fabrics of varying types and weights were used and they seem to have stood the test of time. It is certainly worth experimenting with different weights of fabric, as when used successfully they give new quilts the authentic look of the old quilts.

Right: Apart from the border pieces, this Flying Geese Frame Quilt was made entirely with odds and ends of fabric from Mary's scrap bag.

PROJECT FLYING GEESE FRAME QUILT

REQUIREMENTS

- 25 × 15in (63.5 × 38cm) Paisley fabric
- 30 × 42in (76 × 107cm) border fabric
- Oddments in chosen colour range
- 43 × 49in (109 × 124.5cm) light cotton backing fabric
- 43 × 49in (109 × 124.5cm) cotton, polyester or wool wadding (batting)
- Sewing thread to tone with fabrics
- Quilting thread to tone or contrast with fabrics

THIS QUILT WAS DESIGNED USING INCHES, SO THE METRIC MEASUREMENTS GIVEN HERE ARE APPROXIMATE.

INSTRUCTIONS

1. Copy the following templates from pages 96–99: squares □D, □H and □E; triangles △E, △A, △F and △C; rectangles □B and □C x 2. Label templates for easy identification. On the wrong side of your chosen fabric, draw around the templates to mark the sewing line. Remember to add ¼in (6mm) seam allowance to each piece when cutting out.

2. You will also need the long strips marked A, B and C on Fig 1.

TIP

Where a rectangular template is labelled 'x 2', this means that the short side of the template is placed on the fold of the fabric so that the cut strip is twice the length of the template.

FINISHED SIZE: 40 x 46IN (101.5 x 117CM)

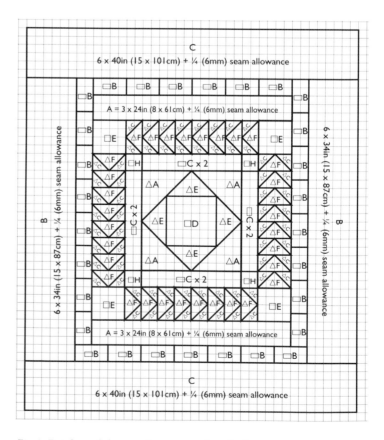

Fig 1. Patchwork layout. 1 square = 1 sq inch

Centre Medallion

1. Attach 4 △E triangles to the keynote ☐D square.
2. Then sew 4 △A triangles to this unit.
3. Sew 2 ☐C x 2 rectangles to the sides of the above and two strips top and bottom, each consisting of 2 ☐H squares and 1 ☐C x 2 rectangle (Fig 2).

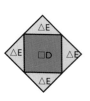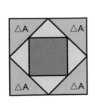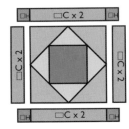

Fig 2.

Flying Geese Borders

1. Make 4 flying geese borders – each border consists of 8 △F triangles and 16 △C triangles formed by attaching 2 △C triangles each side of one △F triangle (Fig 3i).
2. Sew two of these borders to each side of the centre medallion. Then attach 2 ☐E squares to the remaining two borders and sew them to the top and bottom of the centre medallion. Make sure that the geese (the △F triangles) are following each other around the quilt (Fig 3ii).

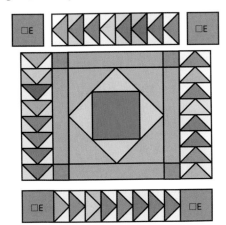

Fig 3i.

Fig 3ii.

3. Cut two pieces (marked A on Fig 1), each 3 x 24in (8 x 61cm), plus ¼in (6mm) seam allowances, and attach them to the top and bottom.

Scrap Rectangle Borders

Make four of these borders:
   – one is made of 6 ☐B rectangles and is attached to the top
   – two are made of 8 ☐B rectangles and are attached to each side
   – the fourth is made of 7 ☐B rectangles and is sewn to the base (Fig 4).

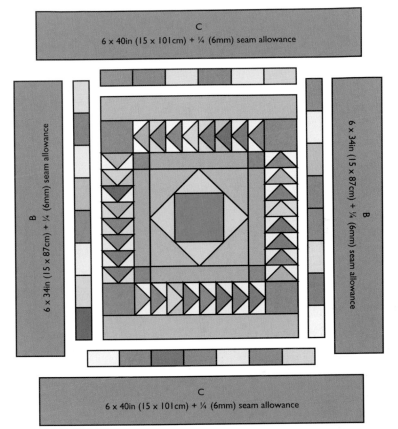

Fig 4.

Outer Borders

1. Cut 2 pieces (B on Fig 1) each 6 x 34in (15 x 87cm) plus seam allowances (see Tip on page 52) and attach them to the sides.
2. Cut 2 pieces (C on Fig 1) each 6 x 40in (15 x 101cm) plus seam allowances (see Tip on page 52) and attach top and bottom.

Quilting and Finishing

1. Press the finished top carefully.
2. Layer the quilt top as described in the general instructions on page 115.
3. Mark out the quilting design following the quilting plan on page 94, or select your own designs from pages 104–112.
4. Complete the quilting following the instructions on page 116.
5. Finish the edge in the traditional butted manner – see page 117.

BRECON STAR QUILT

The design of Brecon Star is based on an old Breconshire quilt typical of the many Welsh quilts made with a central medallion surrounded by randomly pieced strips in a brick-like formation. Although the centres of these quilts usually had a degree of planning, the frames seem to have been assembled without any accurate measuring. If the strips didn't meet, another piece was just added in. Mary has tried to capture this rather thrown-together look in her design but instructions for a spontaneous design can make the working seem complicated. It is far easier to do than to explain! After making the central star, therefore, you may find it easier simply to use the patchwork layout as a guide and try some improvisation. Not only will you be following in the haphazard piecing tradition of old Welsh quilters but the quilt you make will be unique.

Choosing Fabrics

Using chintz in the centre of a quilt was a very common practice (see page 12) but as these fabrics were expensive they were used sparingly. The central star was cut from such a chintz and its colours of red, white and blue dictated the colour scheme, though Mary also added some mauve into the mix. This half-mourning colour was a popular choice for dresses in the 19th century, so pieces left over from dress-making very often ended up in quilts.

In total there are seven different red fabrics, seven blues in dark and medium tones, three mauve medium tones and four different light fabrics. You may want to use the same colour range but if you have a special piece of chintz, you might want to use it as the basis for your own scheme.

Right: Most of the fabrics in the Brecon Star Quilt are vintage Laura Ashley but Mary has also used some that were left over from the blue-and-white Toile de Jouy blinds made for her living room. She feels that using fabrics from everyday life is entirely in the tradition of old Welsh quilt making, when everything was included in the mix.

PROJECT BRECON STAR QUILT

REQUIREMENTS

- ◘ 18 x 18in (46 x 46cm) chintz (or similar) for centre – this will give you some left over to use in the rest of the quilt

- ◘ ½yd (45cm) of four different prints in light, medium and dark tones – these form the borders of the central star (after cutting these borders, there will be plenty left over to use in the rest of the quilt together with other fabrics)

- ◘ Extra fabric scraps or fat quarters in the chosen colour scheme in light, medium and dark tones

- ◘ ⅓yd (122cm) dark print fabric for the border

- ◘ 48 x 51in (122 x 132cm) cotton backing fabric

- ◘ 48 x 51in (122 x 132cm) cotton, polyester or wool batting

- ◘ Sewing thread to tone with fabrics

- ◘ Quilting thread to tone or contrast with fabrics

THIS QUILT WAS DESIGNED USING INCHES, SO THE METRIC MEASUREMENTS GIVEN HERE ARE APPROXIMATE.

FINISHED SIZE: 45 x 48IN (114.5 x 122CM)

TIP

Although this quilt is very haphazard in appearance, the fabric in the middle of the central star was selected using a window template. These are useful for choosing parts of a fabric for a particular effect, and are easy to make. After cutting out the actual template, save the card around it and turn it into a frame which you can then use to select a certain flower or other pattern.

INSTRUCTIONS

1. Copy the following templates from pages 96–99:
   - Squares   □A, □H, □J, □F
   - Triangles   △C, △F
   - Rectangles □C x 2, □D, □E x 2, □F, □J, □K, □L

   Label templates for easy identification. On the wrong side of your chosen fabric, draw around the templates to mark the sewing line. Remember to add ¼in (6mm) seam allowance to each seam when cutting out.

2. You will also need the long strips of fabric marked A, B, C and D on Fig 1.

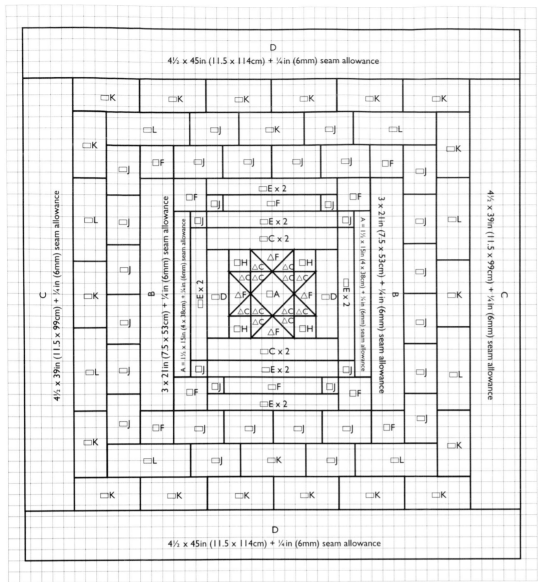

Fig 1. Patchwork layout. 1 square = 1 sq inch

Central Star

1. Sew 4 △C triangles to 1 □A square-on-point to form the central square.
2. Make 4 units of 2 △C triangles sewn to 1 △F triangle.
3. Attach 2 of these to each side of the central square.
4. Add 2 □H squares to each end of the other two and sew these to the top and bottom to complete the central star (Fig 2).

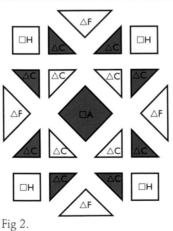

Fig 2.

TIP

Where a rectangular template is labelled 'x 2', the short side of the template is placed on the fold of the fabric so that the cut strip is twice the length of the template.

BRECON STAR QUILT

First and Second Borders

1. Now attach 2 ☐D rectangles to the side of the star and 2 ☐C x 2 rectangles to top and bottom.
2. Add 2 ☐E x 2 rectangles to the side of the above.
3. Make two strips consisting of 2 ☐J squares attached to each end of the ☐E x 2 rectangles and sew these to the top and bottom (Fig 3).

Third and Fourth Borders

1. Cut two strips (A on Fig 1) each 1½ x 15in (4 x 38cm) plus seam allowances, and attach them to the sides.
2. Make two sets of the following and attach them to top and bottom: 2 ☐J squares to each end of an ☐F rectangle and sewn to one ☐E x 2 rectangle. Attach 2 ☐F squares to each end of the above.
3. Cut two strips (B on Fig 1), each 3 x 21in (7.5 x 53cm) plus seam allowances. Attach to the sides (Fig 3).

Scrap Pieced Area

The patchwork layout (Fig 1) should be followed for placement of rectangles and squares. Cut 4 ☐F squares in dark fabric.
Cut the following in assorted colours in light, medium and dark tones and arrange them with reference to Fig 1:
– 24 ☐J rectangles
– 20 ☐K rectangles
– 8 ☐L rectangles.

Final Border

1. Cut 2 strips of border fabric (C on Fig 1) each 4½ x 39in (11.5 x 99cm) plus seam allowances (see Tip). Attach to sides.
2. Cut 2 strips of border fabric (D on Fig 1) each 4½ x 45in (11.5 x 114 cm) plus seam allowances. Attach to top and bottom.

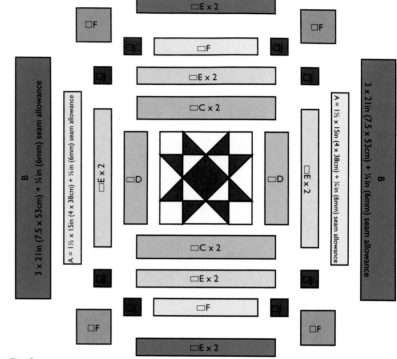

Fig 3.

TIP

When cutting the outer border strips, increase the seam allowance on the outer edge by an extra ¼in (6mm), in order to give a little more fabric to play with when finishing the butted edges.

Quilting and Finishing

1. Press the finished top carefully.
2. Layer the quilt top as described in the instructions on page 115.
3. Mark out the quilting design following the quilting plan opposite, or select your own designs from pages 104–112.
4. Complete the quilting following the instructions on page 116.
5. Finish the edge in the traditional butted manner – see page 117.

PROJECT CARIAD QUILT II

REQUIREMENTS

- ⅔yd (60cm) plain black fabric
- ¼yd (25cm) plain red fabric (cut either as a long or a fat quarter)
- 23 x 23in (58 x 58cm) lightweight wadding (batting)
- 23 x 23in (58 x 58cm) red patterned fabric for backing
- Rotary cutter, self-heal mat and non-slip ruler
- Sewing machine needles, sizes 60 and 70
- Patchwork foot or ¼in (6mm) seam guide
- Open-toed quilting foot
- Fabric marker (light)
- Template plastic
- Freezer paper – small piece approximately 4 x 4in (10 x 10cm) for appliqué
- Black cotton machine thread, eg Sylko 50
- Red thread for appliqué
- Invisible machine quilting thread in 'smoke'
- Black bobbin thread (60)

> THIS QUILT WAS DESIGNED USING INCHES, SO THE METRIC MEASUREMENTS GIVEN HERE ARE APPROXIMATE.

FINISHED SIZE: 21 x 21IN (53 x 53CM)

INSTRUCTIONS

Centre

1. Cut 1 square of black fabric 6½ x 6½in (16.5 x 16.5cm).
   Cut 4 squares of red fabric 3½ x 3½in (9 x 9cm).
   Cut 1 square of red fabric 3 x 3in (7.5 x 7.5cm). HEART

2. Mark a diagonal line from the top left corner to the bottom right on the wrong side of one red square. Place right side down on top of black square. Sew along marked line, trim off corners ¼in (6mm) from seam line and discard. Flip red fabric back and press (Fig 2i and 2ii).

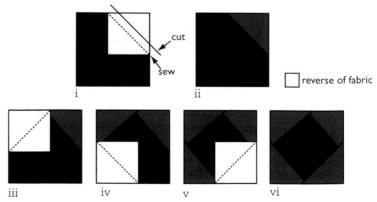

Fig 2. Assembling the square-on-point using Method 1

Fig 1. Patchwork layout

3. Lay second red square right side down on black square, taking care to match raw edges as before and sew across the diagonal (Fig 2iii). Note that the red square will overlap the red triangle slightly. Trim and press.

4. Repeat with remaining red squares to complete centre block (a square-on-point) – Fig 2vi.

5. Trace the heart template (on page 97) on to freezer paper, cut out and press to wrong side of the small square of red fabric. Cut out fabric shape and appliqué by hand to centre of black square-on-point (Fig 3), using the technique described on page 117.

Fig 3.

First Border

1. Cut 1 strip of black fabric 2 x 42in (5 x 107cm).
   Cut 1 strip of red fabric 2 x 42in (5 x 107cm).

2. Join the 2in (5cm) wide strips of red and black fabric with an accurate ¼in (6mm) seam. Press seam allowance towards the black strip. Check the width (3½in or 9cm) of the combined strips and adjust seam allowance if necessary.

3. Cut 4 pieces 6½in (16.5cm) long from this new strip (Fig 4i). Add 2 of these strips to either side of the centre, making sure the black fabric is next to the red of the centre.

4. Cut 8 pieces 2in (5cm) long from the rest of the red-and-black strip and join these in pairs, rotating one piece in each pair as shown in Fig 4iii to form corner blocks.

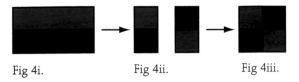

Fig 4i.   Fig 4ii.   Fig 4iii.

5. Add 1 corner block to either end of the remaining 6½in (16.5cm) strips. Alternate the red and black pieces, as in Fig 5.

Fig 5.

6. Add these pieces to the top and bottom of the central block. This completes the first border. Take time to match the intersections of the seams carefully – they should butt together easily if you have sewn an accurate ¼in (6mm) seam.

Second Border

1. Cut 2 strips of black fabric each 5 x 12½in (13 x 32cm).
   Cut 2 strips of black fabric each 5 x 21½in (13 x 55cm).

2. Sew the shorter 12½in (32cm) black strips to the sides of the quilt and press back.

3. Then add the longer 21½in (55cm) strips to the top and bottom to complete the quilt top (Fig 1).

Quilting and Finishing

1. Cut 1 square of wadding (batting) 23 x 23in (58 x 58cm).
   Cut 1 square of backing fabric 23 x 23in (58 x 58cm).

2. Press the quilt top carefully on the wrong side, making sure the seam allowances lie flat.

3. Layer the quilt as described in the general instructions on page 115.

4. Using the quilting plan on page 95, mark the quilting patterns on the quilt top. Alternatively you can plan your own quilting designs using ideas from pages 104–112. Start by outlining the centre and border sections, then place motifs in these areas. Finally add infill.

5. Quilt by hand or machine – see pages 116–117.

6. Finish the quilt with a traditional Welsh butted edge, as described on page 117.

PENNSYLVANIA ECHO QUILT

This simple little quilt, machine pieced and hand quilted by Clare, is a replica of an early Welsh quilt found in America and now in the collection of Ardis and Robert James. Dated 1818 and made of silk and silk-wool, the original is nearly 8ft (2.4m) square. The strong graphic design and subtle dark colours give it an Amish look (though it pre-dates the earliest known Amish quilts by more than 50 years), but the edges are butted, not bound, and it is heavily quilted in the Welsh manner. The quilting designs include a pleasing lily motif and many other more unusual patterns. This greater freedom of design is typical of early Welsh quilts.

Right: The quilting design incorporates natural-looking flowers and ferns combined with traditional spiral and rose motifs. The central double star set in a circle is framed by four handsome lilies. The black borders are also filled with more formal rose and star motifs, while the outer corners contain sunflowers.

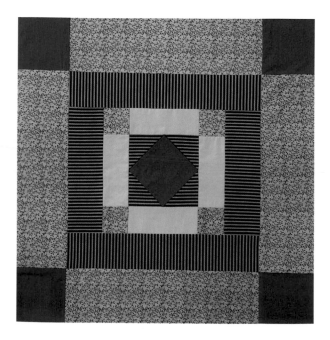

Above: Mary's alternative version of Pennsylvania Echo, which has yet to be quilted, is made using favourite Welsh colours and striped 'petticoat' fabrics.

PROJECT PENNSYLVANIA ECHO QUILT

REQUIREMENTS

- ⬛ ⁷/₈yd (80cm) striped fabric A
- ⬛ ⁵/₈yd (50cm) plain black fabric B
- ⬛ ¼yd (20cm) or a 'fat eighth' of small geometric print or textured fabric C
- ⬛ 36 x 36in (91.5 x 91.5cm) lightweight wadding
- ⬛ 36 x 36in (91.5 x 91.5cm) backing fabric
- ⬛ Rotary-cutting equipment
- ⬛ Sewing machine needle, size 70
- ⬛ Dark cotton machine thread
- ⬛ Fabric marker (light)
- ⬛ Quilting thread to tone with fabrics

THIS QUILT WAS DESIGNED USING INCHES, SO THE METRIC MEASUREMENTS GIVEN HERE ARE APPROXIMATE.

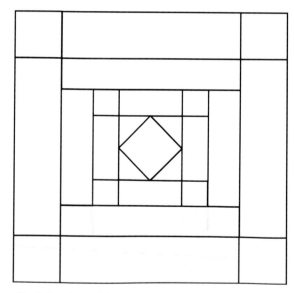

Fig 1. Patchwork layout

TIP

Sometimes it is better to ignore the 'light to dark' rule when pressing seam allowances – the 'square-on-point' block lies much better if the seams go outwards. The fabrics used in the first border are not transparent so there is no problem in doing this.

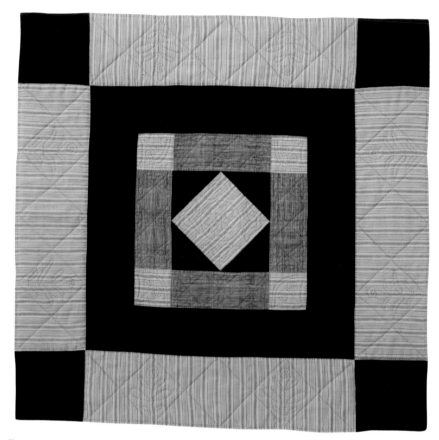

FINISHED SIZE: **34 x 34IN (86 x 86CM)**

INSTRUCTIONS

Centre

1. Cut 1 square of striped fabric A, 6 x 6in (15 x 15cm).
   Cut 2 squares of plain black fabric B, 4⁷/₈ x 4⁷/₈in (12.5 x 12.5cm).
2. Cut each black square in half across the diagonal. Mark the mid-point of the long side of each triangle by folding in half and pinching the crease.
3. Mark the mid-point of each side of the striped square in the same way.
4. Sew a triangle to one side of the square, taking care to match these mid-points. Note that the points of the triangle will project about ³/₈in (9mm) beyond the sides of the square, as in Fig 2i and 2ii. Turn back the triangle and press. Trim away points.
5. Sew the other 3 triangles to the remaining sides of the square in the same way to give a 'square-on-point'. This completes the centre block (Fig 2iii and 2iv).

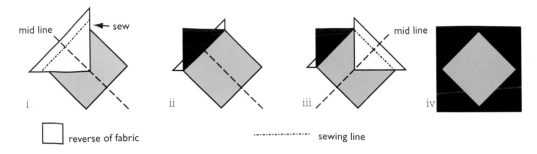

mid line ← sew

□ reverse of fabric   ⋯⋯⋯⋯⋯ sewing line

i   ii   iii   iv

Fig 2. Centre: making a square-on-point using Method 2

First Border

1. Cut 4 rectangles in fabric C, each 3½ x 8½in (9 x 21.5cm).
   Cut 4 squares in plain black fabric B, each 3½ x 3½in (9 x 9cm).

2. Sew 2 rectangles of fabric C to either side of centre block. Turn back and press seam allowance *away* from the centre.

3. Join 1 black square to either end of the remaining rectangles. Press the seam allowance *away* from the black fabric (see Tip, page 70).

4. Add these pieces to the top and bottom of the central block, taking care to match the intersections of the seams carefully. The seam allowances should butt together easily if you have pressed them as recommended. See Fig 3.

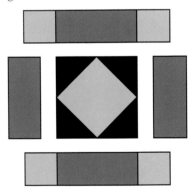

Fig 3.

Second Border

1. Cut 2 strips of black fabric 4½ x 14½in (11.5 x 37cm).
   Cut 2 strips of black fabric 4½ x 22½in (11.5 x 57cm).

2. Sew the 2 short black strips to either side of the centre. Turn back and press seam allowance to one side.

3. Complete the border by sewing the 2 longer black strips to the top and bottom edges.

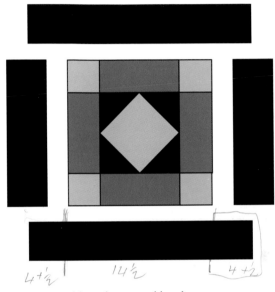

(handwritten annotations: ✗ (OR) cut 4 4½ x 14½ ⊕ 4 x 4½ squares for contrast corners in med. colour)

(handwritten measurements under figure: 4+½   14½   4+½)

Fig 4. Assembling the second border

TIP

When making larger quilts like this one, the lengths of the borders may need adjusting.

1. *Measure the quilt across the centre, not at the edge, and cut the opposing borders to this length.*

2. *Pin the border in place at either end and in the middle, easing in any slight fullness, and sew using a 'walking foot'.*

3. *Turn back these borders and press.*

4. *Re-measure across the full width (quilt top and borders) at the centre and cut the top and bottom borders to this measurement.*

5. *Sew as before. This keeps the quilt 'square' and prevents those wavy edges.*

PENNSYLVANIA ECHO QUILT

Third Border

1. Cut 4 strips of striped fabric A, each
   6½ x 22½in (16.5 x 57cm).
   Cut 4 squares of black fabric B, each
   6½ x 6½in (16.5 x 16.5cm).

2. Sew 2 strips of fabric A to either side of the
   central block. Turn back and press seam
   allowances towards the centre.

3. Sew 1 black square to each end of the
   remaining 2 strips A. Press the seam
   allowances towards the black squares.

4. Join these strips to the top and bottom edges
   of the quilt as for the first border, taking
   care to match the seams at the corners. This
   completes the quilt top (see Fig 5).

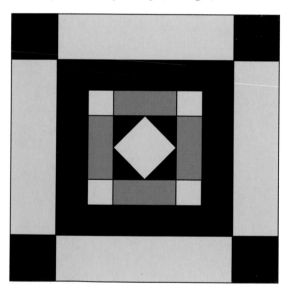

Fig 5.

Quilting and Finishing

1. Cut 1 square of wadding (batting) 34 x 34in
   (86 x 86cm).
   Cut 1 square of backing 34 x 34in
   (86 x 86cm).

2. Press the quilt top carefully on the wrong
   side, making sure the seam allowances lie
   flat. If you plan to quilt over the seam in the
   second border, it may help to nick the seam
   allowances and open the seam flat where the
   black strips join.

3. Layer the quilt as described in the general
   instructions on page 115.

4. Mark out the quilting design on your
   quilt top using the quilting plan opposite.
   Alternatively you could plan your own
   design using ideas from pages 104–112. Refer
   to pages 113–115 for methods of marking.

5. If you are quilting by machine, use a dark/
   smoky translucent thread. If quilting by
   hand, try using a dark, but not black, thread
   that shows up the quilting stitches on all the
   fabrics. Many old quilts were sewn in this
   way – probably out of necessity – but with
   very pleasing results.

6. Finish off the quilt in the traditional way by
   butting the edges – see page 117.

Right: Detail of the
quilting on the second
and third borders.

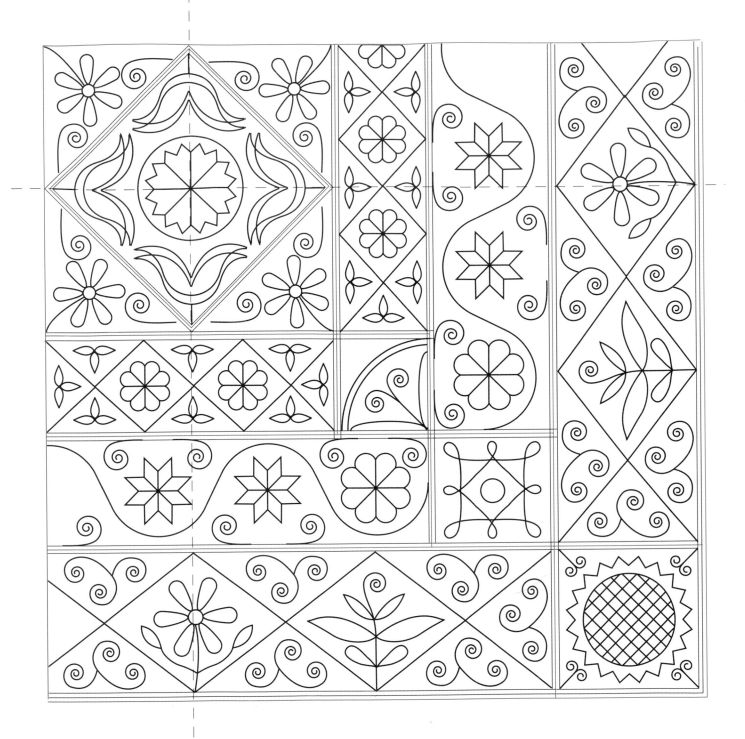

Above: This quilting plan includes the central area and just a little over the quarter-plan, to guide you in marking out the quilting motifs. The red lines indicate the patchwork seams, with the dashed red lines showing the centre line. Clare's replica is much smaller than the quilt that inspired it but she has adapted the quilting motifs of the original quilt, which displays free-flowing themes within geometric borders.

SAWTOOTH QUILT

The inspiration for this quilt was the central section of a late 19th-century wool quilt seen at an exhibition at the Minerva Gallery in Llanidloes in mid-Wales. It came from the collection of Ron Simpson, the quilt collector who lives in the area; another of his quilts is featured in The Quilt Gallery on page 25.

The sawtooth border, in which all the red triangles go anti-clockwise around the central square, gives this simple quilt a great sense of dynamism and enhances its graphic impact.

The original quilt was made of flannel which was produced in the many woollen mills in 19th-century Wales. Unfortunately this industry is now extinct and replica quilts are now made in cotton fabrics.

The elaborate quilting design which Clare has quilted by machine is based on the patterns on the original quilt. It is in the style of Welsh quilting in that the designs are quilted across the boundaries of the patchwork and overlay the outer borders with sweeping curves.

The quilt looks completely at home hung above a pile of logs in the inglenook of an old Welsh cottage, its sawtooth border echoed by the serrated iron pot-hook hanging beside it.

Right: Red, black and grey cotton fabrics have been used in this replica quilt; the original was made of wool flannel. The quilting motifs are based on those of the original quilt.

PROJECT SAWTOOTH QUILT

REQUIREMENTS

- ⅝yd (50cm) plain black fabric
- ¼yd (20cm) or a 'fat quarter' of plain red fabric
- ¼yd (20cm) or a 'fat quarter' of plain light grey fabric
- 28 x 28in (71 x 71cm) lightweight polyester or wool wadding (batting)
- 28 x 28in (71 x 71cm) cotton backing fabric
- Rotary cutter, self-heal mat and non-slip ruler
- Sewing machine needles, size 60 and 70
- Fine (60) dark cotton machine thread
- Invisible machine quilting thread in 'smoke'
- Fabric marker (dark)
- Open-toed quilting foot

THIS QUILT WAS DESIGNED USING INCHES,
SO THE METRIC MEASUREMENTS GIVEN HERE
ARE APPROXIMATE.

FINISHED SIZE: 24 x 24IN (61 x 61CM)

INSTRUCTIONS

Centre

1. Cut 1 square of red fabric 5¼ x 5¼in (13.5 x 13.5cm).
   Cut 4 squares of black fabric 2⅞ x 2⅞in (7.5 x 7.5cm).
2. Mark a diagonal line across each black square on the wrong side of the fabric. This will be your cutting line. Then mark a sewing line ¼in (6mm) either side of this.
3. Lay the large red square right side up on your work surface, then place a black square right side down in the top right-hand corner. Align the edges carefully and sew on the dotted lines (Fig 2i).
4. Cut off the corner 'triangle' and keep this. When pressed open it will form a half-square triangle for use in the second (sawtooth) border.
5. Turn back the black triangle at the corner of the red square (Fig 2ii).
6. Rotate your work clockwise a quarter turn and place a second black square in the top right-hand corner. Sew, cut and press as before (Fig 2iii).
7. Repeat these steps with the remaining 2 black squares and you will have a red square-on-point within a black square which forms the central medallion, plus 4 half-square triangles for use in the sawtooth border (Fig 2v).

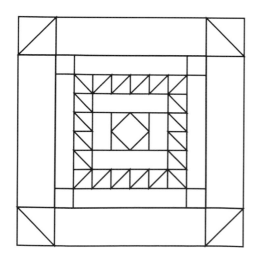

Fig 1. Patchwork layout

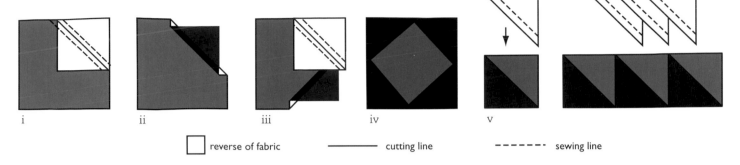

Fig 2. How to make a square-on-point plus 4 half-square triangles

First Border

1. Cut 2 strips of grey fabric, each 2½ x 4½in (6.5 x 11.5cm).
   Cut 2 strips of grey fabric, each 2½ x 8½in (6.5 x 22cm).

2. Sew the 2 shorter strips to either side of the centre square-on-point block. Turn back and press.

3. Add the longer strips to the top and bottom edges to complete the first border (Fig 3).

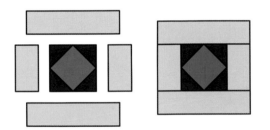

Fig 3. Adding the first border

Second (Sawtooth) Border

1. Cut 8 black squares each 2⅞ x 2⅞in (7.5 x 7.5cm).
   Cut 8 red squares 2⅞ x 2⅞in (7.5 x 7.5cm).

2. Make 16 half-square triangles from the 8 red and 8 black squares as described in Basic Techniques, page 115 (or see Tip, right, for mass production). Add to these the 4 half-square triangles made as by-products of the central square-on-point (see Centre, step 7), making 20 in all.

3. To make up the border strips, arrange them around the quilt centre as shown in Fig 4 and sew together in 2 sets of 4 and 2 sets of 6.

Note how all the red triangles face the same way except those at the ends of the 2 rows of 6, which will be in the top left-hand and bottom right-hand corners of the border.

4. Sew the 2 sets of 4 to the sides of the centre with the red triangles innermost. Then add the 2 sets of 6 to the top and bottom edges.

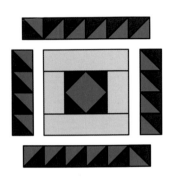

Fig 4. Assembling the second (sawtooth) border

TIP

How to mass-produce half-square triangles

1. *Cut 1 black and 1 red rectangle each 7 x 13in (18 x 33cm).*
2. *Tape red fabric right side down on to your work surface. On the wrong side draw a grid of 2 x 4 squares, each 2⅞ x 2⅞in (7.5 x 7.5cm). Use a non-slip ruler and soft pencil.*
3. *Mark diagonal cutting lines across all the squares, as shown below.*
4. *Lay the red fabric on top of the black with right sides together. Working in a continuous line, sew ¼in (6mm) either side of the diagonals.*
5. *Cut up into individual squares, and then cut these in half and press open. This will give you 16 half-square triangles.*

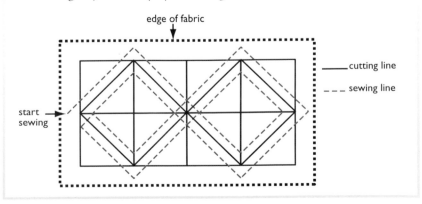

PROJECT SAWTOOTH QUILT

Third Border

1. Cut 4 strips of light grey fabric 2½ x 12½in (6.35 x 32cm).
   Cut 4 squares of red fabric, each 2½ x 2½in (6.35 x 6.35cm).

2. Sew a grey strip to either side of the quilt centre. Turn back and press the seam allowance away from the sawtooth border.

3. Sew a red square to either end of the 2 remaining grey strips, pressing the seam allowance towards the grey fabric.

4. Then attach these to the top and bottom edges of the centre, matching the seams carefully. If you have pressed the seams as directed the pieces should fit together easily.

Fig 6. Assembling the fourth border

Fig 5. Adding the third border

Fourth Border

1. Cut 2 squares each of black and red fabric 4⅞ x 4⅞in (12.5 x 12.5cm). Cut 4 strips of black fabric 4½ x 16½in (11.5 x 42cm)

2. Use the black and red squares to make 4 half-square triangles as described on page 115.

3. Sew a black strip to either side of the quilt, turn back and press the seam allowance away from the centre.

4. Join the half-square triangles made in step 2 to either end of the remaining 2 black strips so that the red triangles face inwards, as shown in Fig 6. Press the seam allowances towards the black strips.

5. To complete the quilt top, sew these borders to the top and bottom edges as shown, with the red triangles pointing inwards and matching the seams carefully as before.

Quilting and Finishing

1. Cut 1 square of wadding (batting) 26 x 26in (66 x 66cm).
   Cut 1 square of backing 26 x 26in (66 x 66cm).

2. Press the quilt top carefully on the wrong side, making sure the seam allowances lie flat.

3. Layer the quilt as described on page 115.

4. Mark out the quilting design on your quilt top with the help of the quilting plan opposite.

5. In order to try to recreate the beautiful sculptured look of the old quilt on the small scale of this project, Clare decided to quilt by machine, using many of the quilting patterns from the original, which was large, made of wool and densely quilted. The patterns did not follow the patchwork but overlaid it and seemed to meld the pieces of fabric together. This effect seemed much easier to achieve with the sewing machine. Use an invisible thread on the top and a fine (60) black cotton on the bobbin.

6. Alternatively, if you prefer to quilt by hand, select some patterns from pages 104–112 and plan your own design.

7. Finish the edges of the quilt by hand or machine in the traditional way with a butted edge as described on page 117.

Above: The quilting plan for this project includes the central area and just a little over the quarter-plan. The red lines indicate the patchwork seams, with the dashed red lines showing the centre lines. Clare has based her patterns on those found in the original Welsh quilt. The simple cartwheel centre is set on a lattice background, which extends over the sawtooth border. These are surrounded by a single deep border of beech leaves, which overlays the two outer patchwork borders. The overlapping arches are filled with a single chain that emphasizes the curves.

PROJECT

PINWHEEL QUILT

The original 19th-century wool quilt that inspired this project came from the collection of Ron Simpson and was first seen at an exhibition at the Minerva Gallery in mid-Wales. It now belongs to The Quilters' Guild of the British Isles, and is featured in The Quilt Gallery on page 31. The design pictured here was machine pieced and hand quilted by Clare. She chose a completely different colourway for her small version of this medallion quilt but tried to remain true to the original quilting designs as far as possible on the reduced scale. The striking patchwork 'wave' border was popular in quilts from this period and the design is echoed in the quilting pattern of the outermost border.

Right: The fresh colours and intricate hand quilting of Clare's Pinwheel Quilt contrast well with an old stone wall in a winter garden.

Above: This is a replica of the original Pinwheel Quilt shown on page 31. It uses Paisley fabric, which was such a feature of old Welsh quilts.

PROJECT PINWHEEL QUILT

REQUIREMENTS

- ⁵/₈yd (50cm) fabric A (blue print)
- ⁵/₈yd (50cm) fabric B (beige/white print)
- 1¼yd (110cm) fabric C (gold print)
- ½yd (40cm) fabric D (black stripe)
- 48 × 48in (122 × 122cm) lightweight wadding (batting)
- 48 × 48in (122 × 122cm) cotton backing fabric
- Rotary cutter, self-heal mat and non-slip ruler
- Sewing machine needle, size 70
- Patchwork foot or ¼in (6mm) seam guide
- Neutral cotton machine thread
- Fabric marker (dark)
- Beige quilting thread
- Hand quilting needles

THIS QUILT WAS DESIGNED USING INCHES,
SO THE METRIC MEASUREMENTS GIVEN HERE
ARE APPROXIMATE.

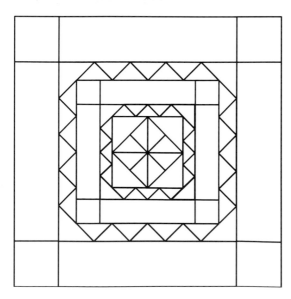

Fig 1. Patchwork layout

TIP

*A good way to stop your fabric from slipping
while drawing the diagonals, is to lay it on
a piece of fine-grained sandpaper.*

FINISHED SIZE: 42 × 42IN (107 × 107CM)

INSTRUCTIONS

Centre Pinwheel Block

1. Cut 1 square of fabrics A and B, each 7¼ × 7¼in (18.5 × 18.5cm). Cut 2 squares of fabric C, each 6⅞ × 6⅞in (17.5 × 17.5cm).
2. Draw in diagonals on the wrong side of the square of fabric B (Fig 2).
3. Place the square of fabric A right side up on your work surface and then lay the square of B right side down on top of A.
4. Starting at the top left-hand corner, sew a seam ¼in (6mm) to the right of the diagonal line as far as the centre. Then, with needle raised, lift the presser foot and move over ¼in (6mm) to the left side of the diagonal and continue sewing to the bottom right corner (Fig 2). Repeat this on the other diagonal.

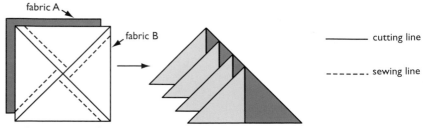

Fig 2. How to make 4 quarter-square triangles

5. Cut along the diagonals to give 4 triangles. Open these out and press the seam allowances towards the darker fabric (A). This will give you four blue-and-beige triangles (Fig 2).

6. Lay one of the squares of fabric C right side up on your work surface. Place two of the blue-and-beige triangles right side down on top (Fig 3). Sew a seam ¼in (6mm) either side of the centre diagonal. Repeat with the second square of fabric C.

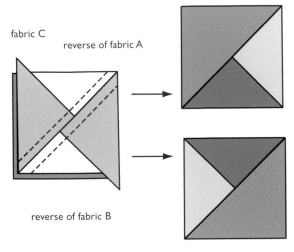

fabric C
reverse of fabric A
reverse of fabric B

Fig 3. Assembling the pinwheel

7. Cut across the centre diagonal on each square and press open. This will give you 4 blocks. Arrange them with the larger triangles facing outwards, as shown in Fig 4. Sew together to give you a blue pinwheel in the centre of your 'four-patch' (see Tip).

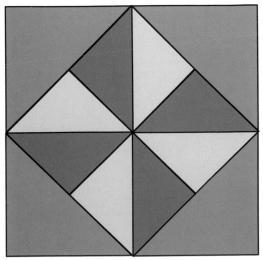

Fig 4.

TIP

Press the seams towards the dark triangles – you will need to tweak a few stitches apart within the seam allowance on the final seam to do this. You will find that the seams arrange themselves in a neat rosette at the centre point.

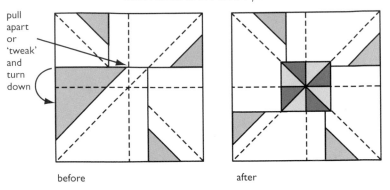

pull apart or 'tweak' and turn down

before   after

First Border

1. Cut 2 squares of fabric A, each 5¼ x 5 ¼in (13.5 x 13.5cm).
   Cut 3 squares of fabric B, each 5¼ x 5¼in (13.5 x 13.5cm).
   Cut 2 squares of fabric A, each 4⅞ x 4⅞in (12.5 x 12.5cm).

2. Cut each of the larger squares of fabrics A and B into 4 triangles across the diagonals.

3. Take 1 light (fabric B) and 1 dark (fabric A) triangle. With right sides together, arrange as in Fig 5i so that the points of the triangles project ⅜in (9mm) at either side. Sew together using ¼in (6mm) seam allowance. When turned back and pressed, the apex of the dark triangle will exactly match the point of the light and vice versa, as shown in Fig 5ii.

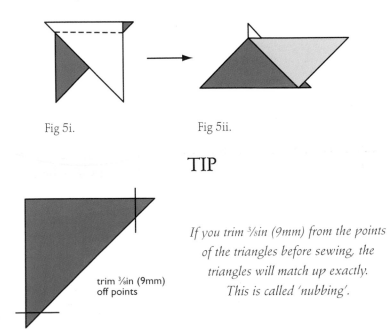

Fig 5i.   Fig 5ii.

TIP

trim ⅜in (9mm) off points

If you trim ⅜in (9mm) from the points of the triangles before sewing, the triangles will match up exactly. This is called 'nubbing'.

PROJECT PINWHEEL QUILT

4. Sew together 4 groups of 3 light and 2 dark triangles. Attach these to each side of the central block as shown in Fig 7, with the dark triangles outermost.

5. Cut the smaller squares of fabric A in half across a diagonal, and sew the 4 triangles in place across the corners ('nubbing' will help to make these triangles fit – see step 4). Turn back and press. This completes the first border.

Fig 7. Joining the first border

Second Border

1. Cut 4 strips of fabric C, each 4½ x 16½in (11.5 x 42cm).
   Cut 4 squares of fabric D, each 4½ x 4½in (11.5 x 11.5cm).

2. Join one strip to either side of the quilt centre. Turn back and press seam allowance outwards.

3. Sew a square of fabric D to either end of the remaining two strips, pressing the seam allowances away from the corner squares. Then sew these strips to the top and bottom edges to complete the second border (Fig 8).

Third Border

1. Cut 3 squares of fabric A, each 7¼ x 7¼in (18.5 x 18.5cm).

Fig 8. Assembling the second border

   Cut 4 squares of fabric B, each 7¼ x 7¼in (18.5 x 18.5cm).
   Cut 2 squares of fabric A, each 6⅞ x 6⅞in (17.5 x 17.5cm).

2. Cut the large squares of A and B into 4 across the diagonals.

3. Assemble as for the first border, using 4 light and 3 dark triangles, and sew around the centre.

4. Cut the 2 smaller squares of A in half across a diagonal and sew these triangles on to the corners as before.

Fourth Border

1. Cut 4 strips of fabric C, each 5½ x 30½in (14 x 77.5cm).
   Cut 4 squares of fabric D, each 5½ x 5½in (14 x 14cm).

2. Assemble this border as for the second border. This completes the quilt top.

Quilting and Finishing

1. Cut 1 square of wadding (batting) 46 x 46in (117 x 117cm).
   Cut 1 square of backing 46 x 46in (117 x 117cm).

2. Press the quilt top carefully on the wrong side, making sure the seam allowances lie flat.

3. Layer the quilt as described on page 115.

4. Using the quilting plan opposite, mark out the quilting patterns on the quilt top. Alternatively plan your own quilting designs using ideas from pages 104–112.

5. Quilt by hand or machine – see pages 116–117.

6. Finish off the quilt in the traditional way by butting the edges as described on page 117.

Above: The quilting plan includes the central section and just a little over a quarter of the quilt. The red lines indicate the patchwork seams with the dashed red lines showing the centre line. The quilting motifs were based on those of the original quilt on page 31. These include a variety of spiral motifs and free-flowing curves surrounded by a wave border.

Making Your Own Welsh Quilts **85**

PEMBROKESHIRE QUILT

This little quilt is based on a large and beautiful chintz quilt in the collection of Jen Jones, which is featured in the Gallery section on pages 12–13. Clare has followed the colour scheme of the original quilt as closely as possible using modern dress-weight fabrics and thus has managed to retain the antique look of the original.

Choosing fabrics to make replica quilts is an interesting as well as challenging process, especially when changing the size of the quilt. One has to search for fabrics that are smaller in scale but with enough detail to replicate the richness and colour placement of the original. Clare found searching for the appropriate small-scale, clearcut and detailed prints for this little quilt a most enjoyable experience.

She suggests that if you want to make a similar antique-looking quilt you should look for a medium-toned 'swirly' print in warm colours and a large-scale light floral print to go with it. With these as the basis of your palette, add one or two darker and lighter fabrics for contrast, and use not one but two accent fabrics like the grey-blue triangles and the pink squares. Try to include a geometric print, like the deep red stripe, and a border print to frame the centre square. Finally, add a border fabric to bring them all together.

These suggested fabrics are only intended as a guide and are not meant to be prescriptive. You may well prefer simply to use the patchwork layout and make a quilt in quite different fabrics altogether. Feel free to use the patchwork layout to devise your own colour scheme, and see what happens!

Opposite: Clare's replica of an original Pembrokeshire chintz quilt from the Jen Jones collection uses modern dress-weight cotton fabrics but nevertheless has an antique look.

PROJECT PEMBROKESHIRE QUILT

REQUIREMENTS

- ⚡ I fat quarter (50 × 50cm) medium-toned swirly print in terracotta with black detail – fabric A

- ⚡ I fat quarter (50 × 50cm) light-toned large-scale floral print – fabric F

- ⚡ ½yd (50cm) medium-toned medium-scale geometric print in terracotta and black – fabric K

- ⚡ Additional fabrics – only small pieces are needed, maximum 12 × 12in (30 × 30cm)
  - delicate white floral print on black – fabric B
  - green-and-beige border print – fabric C
  - dark red-and-brown narrow stripe – fabric D
  - pale pink and white geometric print – fabric E
  - light tan with dark red floral motif – fabric G
  - blue-grey 'accent' print – fabric H
  - terracotta pink and floral print – fabric J

- ⚡ 30 × 30in (80 × 80cm) cotton backing fabric

- ⚡ 30 × 30in (80 × 80cm) lightweight wadding (batting)

- ⚡ Rotary cutter, self-heal mat and non-slip ruler

- ⚡ Fabric marker (dark)

- ⚡ Sewing machine needle, size 70

- ⚡ Quilting needle, size 60

- ⚡ Neutral-coloured cotton bobbin thread (50)

- ⚡ Machine quilting thread in 'smoke'

THIS QUILT WAS DESIGNED USING INCHES,
SO THE METRIC MEASUREMENTS GIVEN HERE
ARE APPROXIMATE.

TIP

When working on a small scale you may find it easier to make accurate half-square triangles if you round up the base squares to 2 × 2in (5 × 5cm) and trim down to the correct size (1½ × 1½in / 4 × 4cm) after sewing.

FINISHED SIZE: 26 × 28IN (66 × 71CM)

Fig 1. Patchwork layout

INSTRUCTIONS

Centre

1. Cut 1 square of fabric A, 7½ x 7½ in (19 x 19cm).
   Cut 4 squares of fabric B, 4 x 4in (10 x 10cm).

2. Make a square-on-point block as described on page 66, using fabric A for the centre and fabric B for the surrounding triangles (see Fig 2).

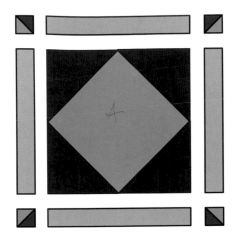

Fig 2.

First Border

1. Cut 1 square of fabric A, 1⅞ x 1⅞in (4.5 x 4.5cm).
   Cut 1 square of fabric D, 1⅞ x 1⅞in (4.5 x 4.5cm).
   Cut 4 strips of fabric C, 1½ x 7½in (4 x 19cm).

2. Make 4 half-square triangles in fabrics A and D as described on page 115.

3. Sew 1 strip of fabric C to either side of the centre block.

4. Sew 1 half-square triangle to either end of the remaining 2 strips, arranging them as shown in Fig 2.

5. Attach the strips to the top and bottom edges of the block to complete the first border.

Second Border

1. Cut 1 square each of fabrics B and H, 3⅞ x 3⅞in (10 x 10cm).
   Cut 8 squares of fabric A, 2⅝ x 2⅝in (6.5 x 6.5cm).

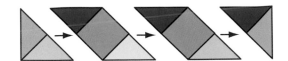

Fig 3i.

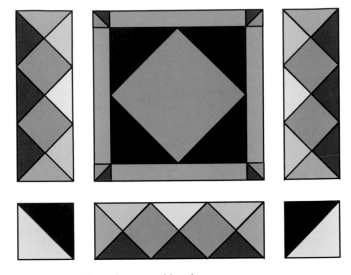

Fig 3ii. Assembling the second border

   Cut 6 squares of fabric D, 3 x 3in (7.5 x 7.5cm).
   Cut 2 squares of fabric E, 3 x 3in (7.5 x 7.5cm).
   Cut 4 squares of fabric F, 3 x 3in (7.5 x 7.5cm).
   Cut 2 squares of fabric G, 4¼ x 4¼in (11 x 11cm).

2. Use the squares of fabrics B and H to make 4 half-square triangles as described on page 115. Set aside.

3. Cut the squares of fabrics D, E and F in half diagonally to make triangles.

4. Cut across both diagonals of the 2 squares of fabric G to give 8 triangles.

5. Now assemble the border units as shown in Fig 3i.

6. Sew 1 border unit to either side of the centre, as shown in Fig 3ii, dark (D) triangles outermost.

7. Sew the half-square triangles made in step 2 to each end of the remaining 2 border units so that the dark (B) triangles point towards the centre of the quilt.

8. Join these borders to the top and bottom edges of the quilt.

Third Border

1. Cut 4 strips of fabric F, each 3½ x 15½in (9 x 39.5cm).
   Cut 4 squares of fabric J, each 3½ x 3½in (9 x 9cm).

2. Sew a strip of fabric F to either side of the quilt centre. Press the seam allowances away from the centre (Fig 4, overleaf).

3. Join a square of fabric J to each end of the remaining two strips of fabric F and press the seam allowances away from the corner squares.

PROJECT PEMBROKESHIRE QUILT

Fig 4. Assembling the third border

4. Sew these borders to the top and bottom edges of the quilt, matching the seams.

Fourth Border

This final border is not symmetrical and makes the quilt rectangular, as in the original. However, if you prefer you can alter the given measurements to retain the square shape.

1. Cut 2 strips of fabric K, each 3 x 21½in (7.5 x 54.5cm). Cut 2 strips of fabric K, each 4 x 26½in (10 x 67.5cm).
2. Sew the narrow strips of fabric K to either side of the quilt (see Fig 1).
3. Sew the wider strips of fabric K to top and bottom edges. This completes the quilt top.

Quilting and Finishing

1. Cut a rectangle of cotton backing fabric, 28 x 30in (71 x 76.5cm).
   Cut a rectangle of lightweight wadding, 28 x 30in (71 x 76.5cm).

2. Press the quilt top carefully on the wrong side, making sure the seam allowances lie flat.
3. Layer the quilt as described on page 115.
4. Using the quilting plan opposite, mark out the quilting patterns on the quilt top. The original quilt shown on pages 12–13 of The Quilt Gallery is heavily quilted with some very beautiful designs including a central vase of flowers. In order to try replicate the designs to scale, and to include as much of the detail as possible, machine quilting in an invisible thread is recommended.
5. Alternatively plan your own quilting designs using ideas from pages 104–112. Quilt by hand or machine, following the instructions on pages 116–117.
6. Finish off the quilt in the traditional way by butting the edges, as described on page 117.

Above: Early 19th-century Pembrokeshire quilts often have very elaborate quilting designs; large flower pots and cable borders are favourite motifs. Clare has designed this quilting plan for her replica, which is actually a scaled-down version of the quilting designs found on the original quilt (see page 12). The plan includes the whole of the central motif, and a little over the quarter-plan for the quilt. The red lines indicate the patchwork seams, with the dashed red lines showing the centre lines.

QUILTING PLANS

The following pages feature the remaining quilting plans from the projects.

Above: The plan shows one-quarter of the whole quilt area, plus the central area of the quilting design for this project. The red lines indicate the patchwork seams, with the dashed red lines showing the centre lines. Hearts are used in the central area and repeated to form an inner border. The spaces around the heart motifs are filled with spirals and small circles. The side borders consist of double spiral motifs and the deeper top and bottom borders have a Church Windows pattern formed by overlapping half-circles which are filled with curved lines and triple spiral motifs.

Above: The plan shows one-quarter of the whole quilt area, plus the central area of
the quilting design for this project. The red lines indicate the patchwork seams, with
the dashed red lines showing the centre lines. A circular design is worked across
the central patchwork medallion which is subdivided to form leaf shapes filled with
lines and spirals. Fan shapes filled with spirals form the four corners and two
borders of spirals complete the rectangle and the outer border of Baptist fans.

Quilting Plans **93**

Above: The plan shows one-quarter of the whole quilt area, plus the central area of the design. The red lines indicate the patchwork seams, with the dashed red lines showing the centre lines. The design has a central motif of four hearts surrounded by swirling Paisley pear and spiral motifs. These are bordered by overlapping circles divided into leaf shapes. The side borders are filled with roses and the top and bottom borders consist of half-circles divided into flower segments and curved lines rather like half a Dresden plate patchwork pattern.

Above: The plan shows one-quarter of the whole quilt area. The red lines
indicate the patchwork seams, with the dashed red lines showing the
centre lines. These patterns are only loosely based on those of the original quilt
because of the great difference in size and because the quilting in the central
medallion completely ignores the appliquéd heart motif. However, the three
borders follow those of the original quilt, with separate motifs in the corner
squares (which solves the problem of turning corners).

PATCHWORK TEMPLATES

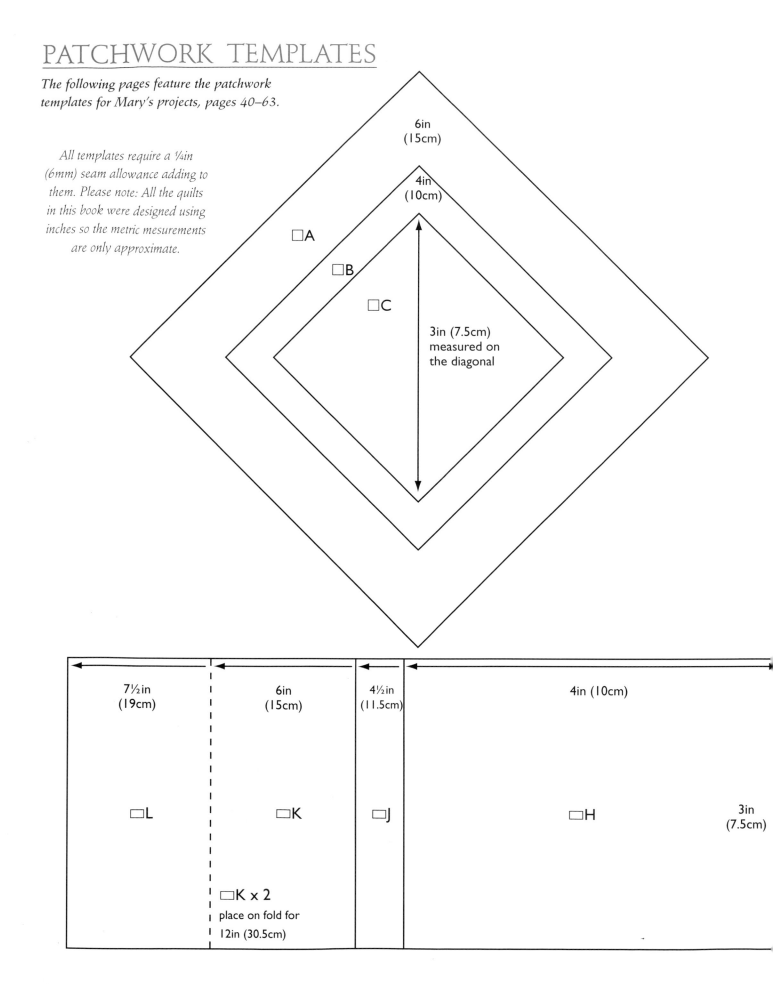

The following pages feature the patchwork templates for Mary's projects, pages 40–63.

All templates require a ¼in (6mm) seam allowance adding to them. Please note: All the quilts in this book were designed using inches so the metric mesurements are only approximate.

6in
(15cm)

4in
(10cm)

☐A

☐B

☐C

3in (7.5cm)
measured on
the diagonal

7½in
(19cm)

6in
(15cm)

4½in
(11.5cm)

4in (10cm)

☐L

☐K

☐J

☐H

3in
(7.5cm)

☐K x 2

place on fold for
12in (30.5cm)

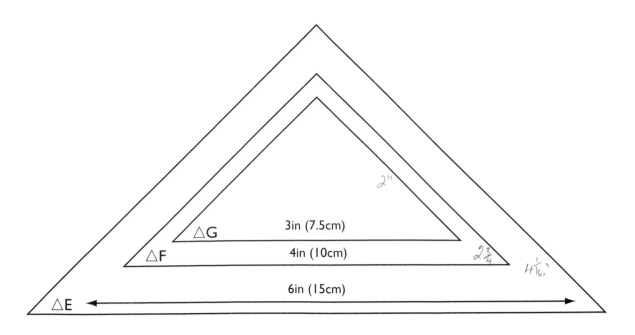

△G   3in (7.5cm)

△F   4in (10cm)

2"

2¾

4¹⁄₁₆"

△E   6in (15cm)

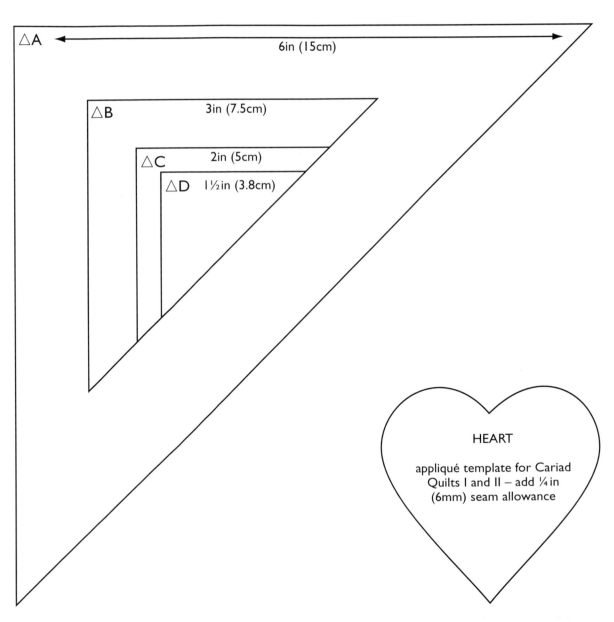

△A   6in (15cm)

△B   3in (7.5cm)

△C   2in (5cm)

△D   1½in (3.8cm)

HEART

appliqué template for Cariad
Quilts I and II – add ¼in
(6mm) seam allowance

PATCHWORK TEMPLATES

All templates require a ¼in (6mm)
seam allowance adding to them.
Please note: All the quilts in this
book were designed using inches
so the metric measurements are
only approximate.

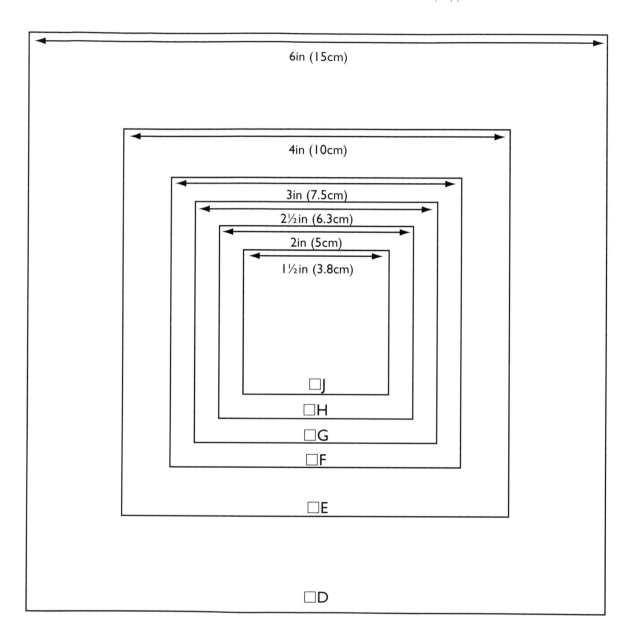

6in (15cm)

4in (10cm)

3in (7.5cm)

2½in (6.3cm)

2in (5cm)

1½in (3.8cm)

☐J

☐H

☐G

☐F

☐E

☐D

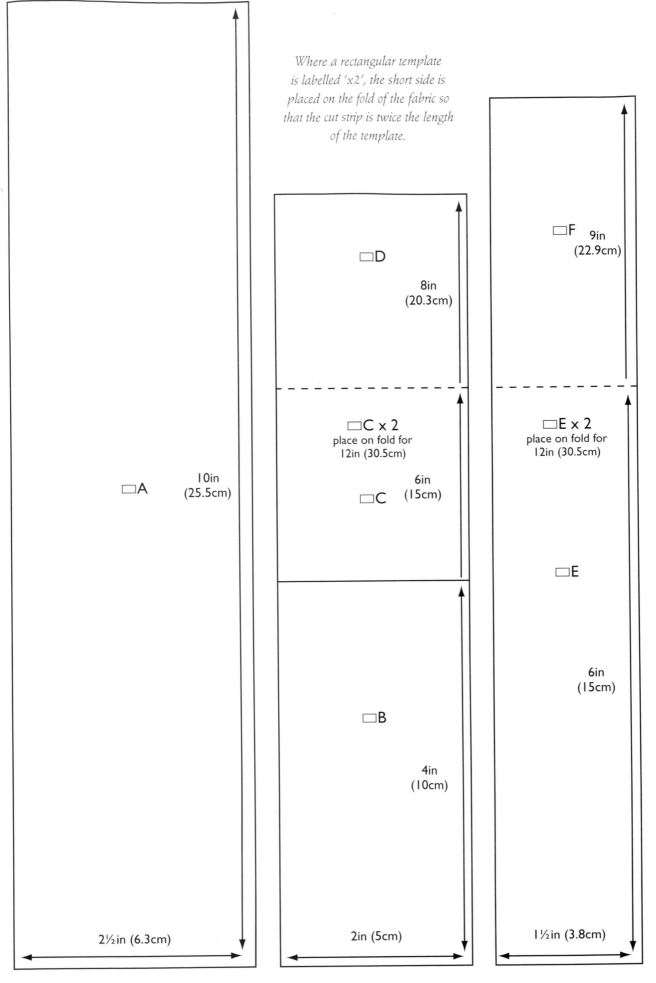

Where a rectangular template is labelled 'x2', the short side is placed on the fold of the fabric so that the cut strip is twice the length of the template.

☐D

8in
(20.3cm)

☐F   9in
(22.9cm)

☐C x 2
place on fold for
12in (30.5cm)

☐C   6in
(15cm)

☐E x 2
place on fold for
12in (30.5cm)

☐A   10in
(25.5cm)

☐E

6in
(15cm)

☐B

4in
(10cm)

2½in (6.3cm)

2in (5cm)

1½in (3.8cm)

WELSH QUILTING

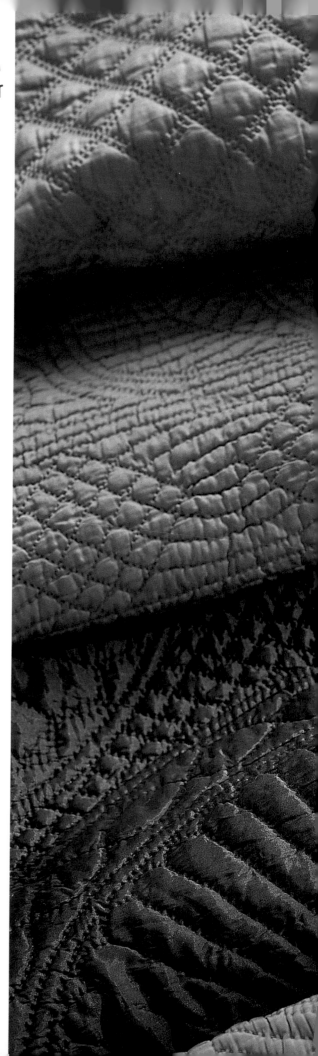

The best Welsh quilting is superb and will hold its own with anything else the quilting world has to offer. The way its patterns were devised encouraged the quilter to be innovative. She knew that she could get out of any difficulties she encountered by imaginative manipulation of motifs, or the twist of a spiral! Welsh quilts are bold, sculptured and free flowing, and there is so little repetition that one feels that the quilter was always trying something different. Each quilt is an intensely personal piece of work, a testament to free expression.

The unique character of Welsh quilting is a combination of the materials used and the imagination and innovation of the quilter. Lambs' wool filling gave the bold sculptured look; the quilting stitches sink into the cloth and create undulations in the surface of the quilt, highlighting its patterns. The sheen of fabrics such as cotton sateen and glazed chintz accentuates this effect. If the quilt top was made of wool, the dyes used, particularly reds and royal-blue, reflected the light in such a way as to give great depth of colour and richness to the quilt surface.

The size of the quilting stitch was not considered as important as it is today. In fact, it was said that too small stitches would give the designs an undesirable harsh outline. So Welsh quilters of old did not pride themselves so much on being able to work a certain number of stitches per inch (though many did achieve very fine work because the carded lambs' wool fleece was so easy to quilt), but on originality of design.

So why is each quilt unique? Why did the quilter take so much trouble over each one? Quilters were professionals with a job to do in a limited time, and their reputation depended on the quality of the work they produced. They weren't highly paid so it would have been understandable if they had taken the easy way by repeating motifs and filling in large areas with cross-hatching or other filling stitches. But these women found time to use elaborate patterns – a precious outlet for creative skills otherwise untapped in their everyday life. Their work is entirely uplifting and anyone who owns one of their quilts is lucky indeed.

We would like you to understand how these quilters worked and how you too can quilt the Welsh way. In doing so we can help to preserve the rich tradition and take it into the 21st century.

Right: A group of cotton and satin 19th and early 20th-century wholecloth quilts. Their wool filling gives them their richly sculptured look.

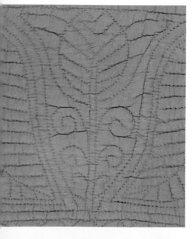

HOW WELSH QUILTERS WORKED

Traditionally Welsh quilters used rectangular wooden frames, which allowed them to develop their designs as the work progressed.

The basic format of a typical Welsh quilt consisted of a square or rectangular central field containing a round or diamond-shaped centre medallion surrounded by one or more borders. The borders were usually delineated by double lines, and had corner squares. On patchwork quilts the borders did not necessarily follow the patchwork seams.

The different areas were often, but by no means always, marked out before the quilt top was put on the frame. The designs were only loosely planned before work commenced.

Most experienced quilters worked in the frame, measuring off the areas either with a long ruler or a chalked string. Ordinary household items, such as cups and plates of various sizes, were then used to draw circles, which were the fundamental units of so many designs. Professional quilters, however, were skilled at using chalk string for drawing circles, arcs and even spirals. For more elaborate motifs they would make their own special templates, and the motifs, and finally the surrounding spaces or background, would then be filled. The quilters were thus able to develop an almost infinite variety of arrangements from simple geometric shapes. Many delighted in using this outlet for self-expression, making their own patterns that were handed down to their family or apprentices. It was a matter of pride not to copy another's designs, and it is possible to identify the work of the best professional quilters by the patterns used.

The beautiful gold quilt pictured opposite was made, according to the inscription in ink on the reverse, in 1905 by Mary Morgans for her brother Stephen. The Morgans family came from rural Cardiganshire (Ceredigon) and the standard of Mary's workmanship suggests that she may well have been a professional quilter. Such women found time between commissions to make quilts for family members and special occasions such as weddings. However, the quilt is in such good condition that it is unlikely to have ever been used, sadly perhaps for Stephen, but fortunately for us.

The overall design of this quilt displays the wonderful mixture of organization and improvisation to be found in Welsh quilts. Mary Morgans was obviously working from right to left along the length of the quilt (bottom right of picture) and had no hesitation in manipulating the pattern when she ran out of room at the other (left-hand) end of the border. Perhaps this should encourage all of us who struggle with design to be more philosophical and less anxious about our mistakes: that way we can relax and enjoy our quilting all the more. Mary's unself-conscious approach gives her quilt great character and charm.

Above: A quilter stands at the quilting frame, placing the templates and marking out the motifs.

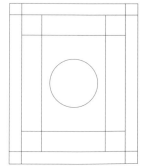

Above: Basic quilt format showing a circular medallion in the middle of a rectangular centre field, surrounded by two borders of differing width and with corner squares demarcated.

Left: Details of flowers, leaves and heart motifs.

WORKING YOUR OWN WELSH QUILTING

You can use Welsh motifs and methods to quilt any piece of patchwork. It is a very practical way of working and you don't need special templates. You can improvise from ordinary cups and saucers, as the old quilters did, but we also show on pages 104–112 how you can draft your own templates to whatever size you wish. After marking out the centre field and the borders, you can then make your own arrangements of the motifs such as leaves, fans, hearts and waves. Once you have stitched the outline of a motif you can choose from a variety of infills to embellish them before finally completing the background. The quilting design then develops as the work progresses and you are free to make changes as you go along, which is what gives every quilt its own character.

If you haven't done anything like this before, you need to be bold in your approach. Marking and quilting across the boundaries of the patchwork is foreign territory to most hand quilters. But the results will surprise and please you as it seems to enhance the patchwork, giving it a richer and more textured appearance.

MOTIFS AND QUILTING PLANS

In the following pages each of the principal motifs found in Welsh quilts is described and examples of their usage shown. A number of borders and infills are also illustrated; these are frequently used in Welsh quilts but are not necessarily exclusive to them. It would be impossible to include templates for all the quilting designs used in this book, but information on drafting them is given, in the form of diagrams, in each of the relevant sections.

Quilting plans are given for each of the projects if you need guidance; however, we hope you will feel inspired to try out your own unique combination of Welsh quilting designs.

PATTERNS HEARTS

The heart motif appears constantly on Welsh quilts in the late 19th century and early 20th century, and it is often assumed this denoted a marriage quilt. Certainly, the finely worked 'best' quilts that featured heart motifs were made as part of a Welsh girl's dowry. However, hearts were used so extensively that this cannot always have been the case, though it would be nice to think that it signified that they were at least made with love.

The heart is an attractive and useful shape because of its combination of curved and straight sides. The central space can be filled with a great variety of patterns and the basic motif is easily adapted to fit into corners and spaces.

It is easy to draft your own heart motif to any size, following the diagram below.

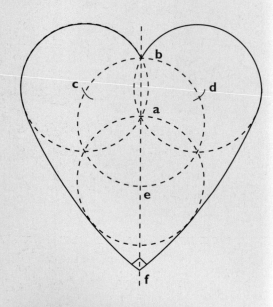

HOW TO DRAFT A HEART

1 Draw a vertical line at least twice the height of the desired motif. Mark a point *a* on this line and draw a circle with a radius one quarter the width of the heart, with *a* at the centre.

2 From point *b*, where the circle cuts the line, mark two points *c* and *d*, and draw two more circles with *c* and *d* as their centres.

3 Draw a fourth circle with its centre at point *e*, where the first circle cuts the vertical line. Draw two lines from the edges of circle *e* to *f* on the vertical line, making a right angle.

4 Now draw the outline of the whole heart around the circles, as shown.

A selection of heart motifs with various infill designs

Designs for centre medallions using hearts

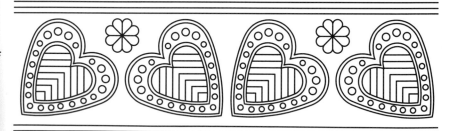

Heart designs for borders

PATTERNS PAISLEY OR WELSH PEAR

The Paisley design is one of the best known motifs from Welsh quilts, but did not become popular until the early 19th century.

At the end of the 18th century, Kashmiri shawls were essential fashion accessories. By the 1820s, imitation shawls were being produced by weavers in Paisley, Scotland, so the 'boteh' or pear-shaped motif copied from the Kashmiri weavers (who had been influenced by Persian designs) became known as the 'Paisley pear'. In Wales, where old shawls were cut up for patchwork, the motif became so popular that it was renamed the 'Welsh pear'.

The motif appears to have been drawn free-hand and so varied greatly in form, from the original 'boteh' with a hooked tip, to a more rounded pear, and ultimately to a pointed teardrop. The last was often given a leaf-like vein infill.

It is easy to draft your own pear motif, to any size, following the diagram below.

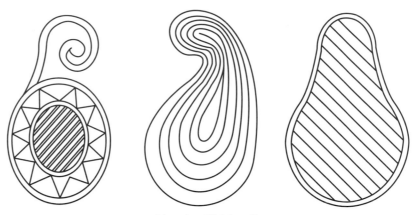

Variations on the Paisley motif found in Welsh quilts

Designs for centre medallions using teardrops

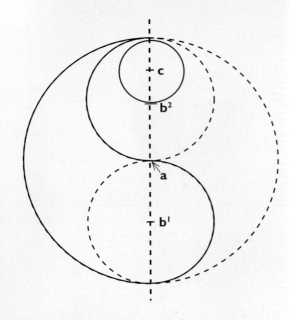

HOW TO DRAFT A WELSH PEAR

1 Draw a vertical line a little more than the height of the desired motif. Mark a point *a* on this line and draw a circle with a radius half the height of the finished motif, with *a* at the centre.
2 Now draw two circles within the first, each with a radius half that of the first, with b^1 and b^2 as their centres.
3 Halve the radius again and draw a circle with its centre at *c*.
4 Now draw the pear's outline as shown.

Border design using Paisley or Welsh pear

Teardrop design for borders

PATTERNS LEAVES

Leaf designs have always been favourites with Welsh quilters. Many were taken directly from nature and are easily recognizable, such as ivy, oak, horse-chestnut and beech, while others are stylized versions and some are entirely original.

The beech leaf was used as a centre motif, in borders and in corner squares, its simple form lending itself to a variety of combinations and infills. Both beech and laurel leaves are easily drawn from overlapping circles (see below).

Bent leaves were also very popular. They were frequently used in the centres and wide borders of the older quilts, and also in odd spaces in later, less sophisticated quilts.

Large and very striking 'twisted' leaves were found in wide borders throughout the 19th century. Smaller versions were used in mirrored pairs, often together with a central oval 'bud' shape making a motif called the 'tulip' (see page 107), which was very popular.

Small leaves such as the ivy and clover or trefoil appear as infill amongst larger border motifs in much the same way as small spirals and hearts.

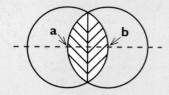

HOW TO DRAFT A BEECH LEAF

1 Draw a line and mark a point *a*.
2 From *a*, draw a circle with a radius to match the desired width of leaf.
3 Draw a second circle with the same radius from *b* (where the first circle bisects the line).
4 The leaf is formed where the circles overlap.
5 A narrower laurel leaf can be created by drawing the second circle further along the line so that there is less overlap.

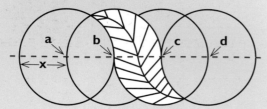

HOW TO DRAFT A TWISTED LEAF

1 Draw a circle, radius *x*, from point *a* (*x* is equal to half the height of the leaf).
2 Draw a second circle of the same radius from point *b* where the first circle bisects the line.
3 Draw two more circles from points *c* and *d* as shown. Fill in the shaded area to form the twisted leaf shape.

Bent leaf

Maple leaf

Twisted leaf

Designs for centre medallions using leaves

Border of laurel leaves and spirals

Border of twisted leaves

PATTERNS FLOWERS

$\mathcal{S}$plendid arrangements of fantasy flowers in urns graced the centre of many early chintz quilts, such as the one shown on page 12.

A selection of flower designs from some of the early Welsh quilts are shown here. On later quilts the representations of favourites, such as the rose, the tulip, the daisy and the sunflower, became stylized.

The most common flower motifs were based on circles drawn with a piece of chalk on the end of a length of string, or by tracing around a plate, and then card templates would be made for the individual petals. Smaller versions of flowers such as roses or daisies, which were often used as infill, were drawn freehand and squeezed into awkward spaces.

Many beautiful and elaborate border designs were made from combinations of flowers and large leaves. Tulips were extremely popular. These were made by combining two 'twisted' leaves with an oval centre. But the rose was the favourite flower of all, expanding to fill central medallions and used in corner blocks and as border motifs.

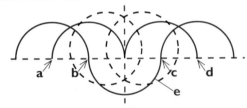

HOW TO DRAFT A TULIP

1 Draw two pairs of four overlapping half-circles, radius x, above the line from points a, b, c and d, as shown. Add another below the line at point e.
2 Shade in the areas shown to form the outer petals of the tulip.
3 The centre of the flower is made using the beech leaf template (see page 106), positioned centrally, where the two blue circles overlap.

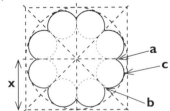

HOW TO DRAFT A ROSE

1 Draw a square and divide it into eight equal sections, as shown.
2 Draw a circle a radius x half the length of one side of the square, to touch the sides of the square. Then draw a second smaller circle inside the first.
3 In each section of the inner circle, draw a curve from a to b through c on the outer circle.

Fantasy flowers in an urn

Rose centre medallion

A selection of fantasy flower designs

Border of mixed flowers ('pinks') from a Gwent quilt

Border from an early 19th-century chintz quilt, owned by Jen Jones

PATTERNS SPIRALS

The spiral is one of the most characteristic motifs of Welsh quilts, giving a flowing quality to the designs. It is added as a flourish at the end of leaf motifs, suggests the unfurling tip of a fern, becomes part of many complex flower arrangements, (see diagrams, right), and contributes to the free-flowing lines of the more naturalistic patterns found in the early Welsh quilts (see the Pennsylvania Echo Quilt plan, page 73). It is much more than 'just an infill', although in practical terms it seems made for this role, capable of being drawn any size and distorted to fit almost any space.

A selection of spiral designs is shown here. Special mention should also be made of the Welsh scissors or shears (see page 19) and the ram's head, both of which would have been very familiar to the country needlewoman. The diagram below shows how to draft a large spiral – but small spirals were mostly drawn freehand – so take your courage in both hands and have a go!

A selection of simple spirals *Asymmetrical spiral*

Dandelions *Ram's head* *Welsh scissors*

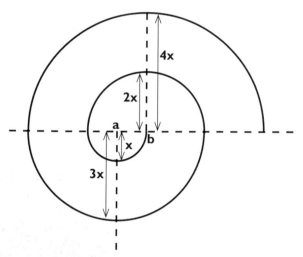

HOW TO DRAFT A LARGE SPIRAL

1 Draw a horizontal line and mark centre a. Draw a semicircle below the line with radius x from this point.
2 From point b where the arc meets the horizontal line, draw another semicircle with a radius of $2x$ above the line.
3 Draw a third semicircle below the line from a, with a radius of $3x$.
4 From point b draw aa fourth semicircle above the line with a radius of $4x$.
5 Carry on in this way until the spiral reaches the required size.

Three narrow borders using spiral motifs

Impressive wide border of large spirals

PATTERNS FANS AND CIRCLES

In the later 19th- and early 20th-century Welsh quilts the central medallion was almost always a circle and the circle was the fundamental element for drafting most quilting patterns. They were usually surrounded by a circular double frame and set off by a simple background infill of diamonds. In addition, the corners of the centre field were often filled with quarter circles or fans matching the centre design, thus making a spectacular focal point for the quilt as it lay on the bed. Occasionally fans were used as the central design of a quilt.

Double fans or half-circles were often used in borders – perhaps the best known being Church Windows. The interesting spaces of this design, made by the overlapping half-circles, provided limitless opportunities for different combinations of traditional infill patterns and motifs.

Templates for the smaller circles were most likely to be improvised from plates and cups (the wineglass gives its name to a pattern), but of course could be drawn with a compass and cut out in card. Professional quilters drew circles with a piece of chalk tied to a length of string in the traditional and highly accurate manner. The popular 'wave' border, or Baptist fan, was also marked in this way, or with chalk held in the hand, using the elbow as a pivot.

Spectacular corner fans

Circle design known as Abertridwr Star   *Centre diamond with fans and circles*

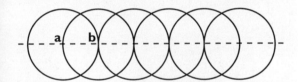

HOW TO DRAFT PATTERNS FROM OVERLAPPING CIRCLES

1 To fill a border with overlapping circles, draw a horizontal line through the middle of the border and mark a point *a*.

2 Draw a circle from *a*, with a radius approximately half the desired width of the border.

3 Draw a second circle from point *b* where the first circle bisects the line.

4 Leaves, arches and other shapes will 'appear' as you continue.

Two other designs are shown here (wineglass left, crank right) which are made by drawing circles from the corner of the square, and from the mid-point of each side.

Border design using fans

Church Windows border

PATTERNS BORDERS

The borders of Welsh quilts were never an afterthought, as in some modern quilts, but an intrinsic part of the whole design, and just as elaborate as the central medallion. Typically, one or more borders of different widths were delineated by double lines of quilting. In early chintz quilts from West Wales a twisted cable was often used and the borders of Mary Morgans' quilt on page 103 were marked out by rows of spirals. The number of borders would depend on the width of the designs, extra narrow borders being added to make up to the required size. Usually, a square at each corner of the border would contain a separate, contrasting motif. This solved the problem of 'turning the design' through a right-angle and added a greater variety of pattern. Sometimes a 'half border' was inserted to convert the quilt shape from square to rectangular in the same way as the patchwork tops (see the Summer Quilt design on page 44). Depending on the drafting skills of the quilter, motifs sometimes had to be distorted and 'squashed in', or left incomplete.

A variety of simple narrow borders are shown here. Almost all of these depend on simple arrangements of curved or straight lines – circles, semicircles, arcs and triangles – forming chains, cables, overlapping arches (known as Church Windows), waves, chevrons and diamonds.

Mention has already been made of the design made from overlapping arches and known as Church Windows. When used in the wide borders this offered great scope for lavish embellishment and was a great favourite with Welsh quilters.

Another lovely design called the Welsh Trail can be seen on the quilting plan for Cariad Quilt II on page 95. It is based on a modified cable – the instructions opposite show how to draft it.

In the wide borders of Welsh quilts a much greater variety of motifs was used. By combining two or more motifs such as hearts, flowers and leaves, and using different types of infill, complex and highly decorative borders were created.

CREATING A BORDER

If you feel inspired to create your own unique border for a project, follow the instructions opposite. Then choose your own combination of infill patterns to complete the motif.

Single chain

Double chain

Triple chain

Simple Welsh Trail

Triple Welsh Trail

Church Windows

Beehive

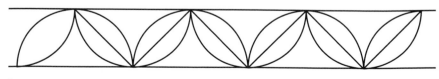

Leaves

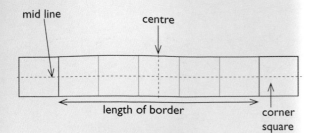

mid line   centre

length of border

corner square

HOW TO DRAFT A BORDER

1. Find the centre point of the border and also mark the mid line to ensure your quilting will be central.
2. Divide the space between the corner squares into equal sections, starting from the centre working outwards.
3. Mark the divisions on to your quilt to allow you to mark the border design accurately.

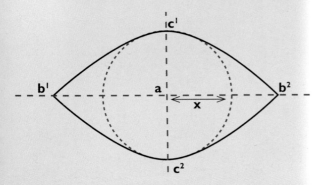

c^1

b^1 a b^2

x

c^2

HOW TO DRAFT A CABLE OR CHAIN

1. Draw a line horizontally through the centre of your border and mark a point a on the line.
2. Draw a circle from this point, with radius x equal to half the desired width of the border.
3. Mark points b^1 and b^2 at equal distances on either side of the circle.
4. Draw a curve above the mid-line from b^1 through c^1 to b^2.
5. Repeat below the line to complete the template.

 By varying the distance of b from the centre of the circle, the curve of the 'chain link' can be altered; the links may also be overlapped as shown below to produce a cable effect.

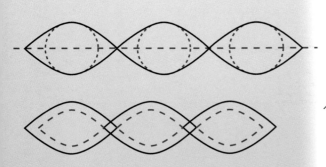

Using the cable template to draft a border

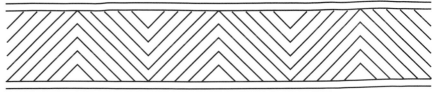

Wave border

Two different diamond borders

Two chevron borders designed by Emiah Jones

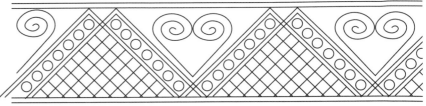

Lala Leach's 'pennies and hearts' border

PATTERNS INFILLS

The infill of quilting motifs and the background between them was an essential part of a Welsh quilt's design. Absolutely no space greater than 1in (2.5cm) could be left unquilted because it was the stitching that prevented the wool-fleece filling from shifting during use, especially during washing.

However, both country quilters and professionals seldom took the easy way by working simple lattice patterns. With the exception of the background of the centre field which was kept deliberately simple to offset the elaborate central medallion, great imagination and ingenuity was employed in filling these spaces, adding greatly to the character of a quilt and often becoming a way of 'signing' it. The work of many of the old quilters or their apprentices could be easily identified by the combinations of motifs and infills used.

The simplest types of infill found are not specific to Wales, but the wave, shell and wineglass patterns were particular favourites. In addition, small hearts, roses, stars, teardrops and of course the spiral, were used with great enthusiasm and imagination.

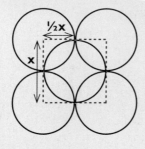

HOW TO DRAFT THE WINEGLASS PATTERN

1 Divide the space or 'field' you wish to fill into a square grid, side length x – see red lines on the diagram. Tip: It is best to start at the centre and draw outwards, so that the edges can be adjusted to fit.

2 Draw a circle, radius $\frac{1}{2}x$ from each intersection of the grid. The overlapping circles thus formed make the wineglass design (so-called because a glass was often used as the template). An infill pattern can be created from this following the diagram below.

Square on point lattice   Square lattice   Double diagonals

Diamond lattice   Waves

Baptist Fans   Wineglass   Clamshell

Star   Spiral   Paisley

Heart   Trefoil

Crank   Rose

BASIC EQUIPMENT

If you are new to patchwork, we refer readers to some of the many excellent specialist books available – see Bibliography, page 118. Each project contains the specific information necessary to make the particular quilt, with fabric quantities, notes on the fabrics used, a patchwork layout, assembly diagrams and a quilting plan. Templates for the hand-pieced projects are given on pages 96–99.

The fabric requirements assume that the width of the fabric is a minimum of 42in (107cm). In the rotary-cut projects an allowance of 3–4in (7.5–10cm) is made for straightening the edges of the fabric. If you are unsure that you have enough fabric, prepare a trial layout of your pieces, starting with the largest ones first, on squared paper or directly on your fabric using tailor's chalk and a ruler.

Drawing and Template-Making

Pencils, 2H and 2B

Ruler

Set-square

Pair of compasses

Graph paper – imperial or metric

Template plastic (clear) or medium-weight card

Glue stick

Scissors for cutting card, plastic and paper

Fine-grained sandpaper (to hold fabric while drawing around templates)

'Add-a-Quarter' ruler

Hand-Sewing and Quilting

Fabric shears

Thread snips

Fine flat-headed pins

Cotton sewing thread 40

Needles – sharps sizes 8–10

Thimble

Fabric markers (for light and dark fabrics)

Quilt pins

Light-coloured thread and long needle for basting

Quilting thimble and an 'under' thimble for the index finger of the underneath hand

Waxed quilting thread, eg YLI or Corticelli

Betweens or quilting needles sizes 8–10

Hoop or traditional rectangular frame

Machine Sewing and Quilting

Needles – 70 (universal and quilting)

Machine thread – 50 cotton for piecing, neutral light and dark, eg sand and grey

Patchwork foot – gives automatic ¼in (6mm) seam allowance from outer edge of foot to needle (alternatively use a double layer of ¼in (6mm) masking tape as a seam guide)

Straight stitch throat plate – improves the stitch when sewing straight seams and quilting

Dual-feed or walking foot – for long seams and when outline quilting (quilting 'in the ditch')

Darning foot or large quilting foot for free-motion quilting

Invisible nylon thread (clear or smoke) for top and 50 cotton for bobbin when quilting

Quilting gloves or rubber finger-stalls – to help you grip the quilt when free-motion quilting

Safety pins and a teaspoon for pin-basting prior to machine-quilting

Rotary Cutting

Rotary cutter (45mm) – push-start type recommended

Self-heal cutting mat (double-sided industrial quality)

Acrylic non-slip ruler 6 × 18in (15 × 40cm) and 8½in (21cm) square – Creative Grids, for example, make a range of good-quality non-slip rulers and squares in both imperial and metric versions

Quilt Marking

There is a huge variety of tools on the market for quilt marking and you will probably need more than one sort for different tasks. Some of the oldest and simplest are best:

Tailor's chalk or a chalk wheel in blue and white for marking light and dark fabrics

Soap – the small slivers of simple soap that always get left by the rest of the family, when dried for a week or so provide a fine edge for drawing which is fabric friendly

More modern alternatives are:

Soapstone pencil (for dark fabrics)

Graphite pencil (for light fabrics)

Light toned watercolour pencils

Whichever method you choose, always mark sparingly and use a pencil sharpener or craft knife to keep a fine sharp point or edge.

BASIC TECHNIQUES

FABRIC PREPARATION

All fabrics should be pre-washed and ironed to check for colourfastness and shrinkage. However, if the finished item is to be used as a wall-hanging and will not need washing, you can omit this step. In fact the 'dressing' in new fabrics will help protect them from dust and dirt.

If you wish to go for the 'antique' look, use a natural wadding (batting), eg cotton, and do not pre-wash the fabrics and wadding. The differential shrinkage that occurs when the finished item is washed produces the wrinkled appearance of an old quilt.

MAKING TEMPLATES

Copy the required templates from pages 96–99 on to template plastic, or photocopy and paste on to lightweight card. Label the templates carefully and mark the fabric grain lines. Then trace around the templates with a soft (2B) pencil on the wrong side of the fabric. Hold the fabric in place on fine-grained sandpaper while you draw. Be sure to add ¼in (6mm) seam allowance before cutting out, using an 'Add-a-Quarter' ruler or similar.

HAND PIECING

With right sides together, pin your pieces at right-angles to the edges, matching the drawn lines carefully. Using a 'sharps' needle and 40 cotton, sew with a small running stitch and an occasional backstitch along the drawn seamline. Start and finish with a double backstitch at the exact end of the seamlines – there is no advantage in sewing into the seam allowance. When crossing seams, leave the seam allowances free. Stitch as close to the seam as possible, then pass the needle through the seam allowances to the other side and continue stitching on the drawn line.

Below: Detail of the Brecon Star Quilt on pages 58–63, showing hand-pieced patchwork.

ROTARY CUTTING

If you are new to the technique, refer to a specialist book such as *Measure the Possibilities with Omnigrid* (see Bibliography page 118), which gives detailed instructions.

Remember, rotary cutting is fast and very accurate if you get the basics right, so time spent in preparing your fabric and making the first cut is never wasted!

Rotary cutting tips

- Fold fabric in half lengthways, taking care to match the selvedges, and press the fold, making sure there are no wrinkles.

- Place on the self-heal mat with the fold towards you and the raw edge to your right (if you are left-handed reverse this). Lay the non-slip ruler at right-angles to the fold, close to the raw edge, and trim away the surplus. Check that the cut edge does not dip at the fold, which indicates the cut was not exactly at right-angles: if it does, re-align the ruler with the aid of a set-square and cut again. You are now ready to cut strips of the required widths for your project.

- If you need rectangles and triangles of varying size, it helps to cut your first strip the full width of your fabric and as wide as the biggest pieces. Cut off the shapes you need, then trim down the remaining strip to the width of the next size you need, and cut off these. Continue in this way until you have all the pieces you require in that particular fabric. Note that you may need to cut more than one strip. This method is particularly useful for cutting individual squares and the short strips of different widths that are needed for the small quilts in the projects.

- Note also that the lines marked on your ruler have their own width, albeit very small, so when you position your ruler to cut strips, make sure that the fabric reaches the outer edge of the line – it is easy to trim down pieces that are slightly too big, but the reverse is not possible!

- The dimensions in all of the rotary-cut and machine-sewn projects in this book include seam allowances. Therefore when you machine the pieces together it is very important to sew accurate ¼in (6mm) seams. A patchwork foot is very valuable for this, or you could make your own seam guide on your machine bed with two or three layers of ¼in (6mm) masking tape laid parallel to a general-purpose foot.

MACHINE PIECING

Piecing patchwork by machine is a relatively fast process provided you are up to speed on the technique. If you are new to it, refer to *Quilting from Start to Finish* (see Bibliography, page 118).

Machine piecing tips

- Use a slightly shorter stitch than normal on your machine so that threads unravel less easily.

- To sew ¼in (6mm) seams accurately, use a special patchwork foot or lay a piece of masking tape across the machine bed exactly ¼in (6mm) away from the needle and use this as a guide.

- To save thread, fold a scrap of waste fabric in half and place under the machine foot. Sew a few stitches to anchor the threads and then feed the fabric pieces, right sides together, under the foot. At the end of the seam feed another small folded piece of fabric under the foot to anchor the threads again. This also prevents a tangle of threads on the reverse.

- When stitching a number of small identical units, feed them under the needle one after another without cutting the thread and use the above tip to finish off at each end of the 'chain'. Transfer the chain to the ironing board for pressing and then snip apart.

- When you are adding borders to a quilt top you may need to pin them. Use flat-headed pins and place them at right-angles to the fabric edge. With care most machines will stitch over the pin or you can pull the pin away just in front of the foot. Using a 'dual-feed' or quilting foot helps to prevent the fabrics from slipping.

FAST-PIECING

This technique is used in the Sawtooth Quilt (pages 74–79) and the Pembrokeshire Quilt (pages 86–91) projects.

How to make half-square triangle blocks:

1. Place two squares of fabric right sides together on your work surface, with the wrong side of the lighter fabric uppermost.
   Note: you need to add ⅞in (2.2cm) seam allowance to the finished size of the block.
2. Mark a line across from the top left corner to the bottom right, using a soft pencil, fabric pen or chalk pencil.
3. Then sew ¼in (6mm) on either side of the marked line.
4. Cut along the marked line and separate the triangles.
5. Open out and press to make two half-square triangles.

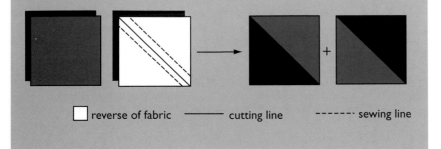

☐ reverse of fabric ——— cutting line ------ sewing line

PRESSING

Literally press your fabrics; do not iron, as this can stretch and distort them. Dry-press each seam as you sew: first press the seam line to set the stitches, then press the seam allowance to one side, light to dark where possible. Press seam allowances of adjoining pieces in opposite directions, so that they butt together neatly when sewn.

Steam-press only when the quilt top is complete. Clip any loose ends of thread, and trim any dark seam allowances that show through lighter patches on the right side. Press carefully from the back, first making sure that the seam allowances lie flat. Then turn the top right side up and pin to the ironing surface and steam-press again. Leave the quilt top in place on the ironing board to cool. This helps 'set' the fibres.

PREPARATION FOR QUILTING

Press the backing fabric and allow the wadding (batting) time to expand to its full loft if it has been compressed in storage. Cut your backing and wadding (batting) 4in (10cm) larger than the quilt top. For the smaller projects, 2in (5cm) extra (1in / 2.5cm larger all round), will be adequate.

Fold the backing in half to find the centre. Lay right side down and hold in place with masking tape or spread out and pin with heavy-duty quilt pins. Spread the wadding (batting) out on top of this. Then place the quilt top right side up on top of that, taking care to match the centres. Using a large needle and pale thread, start tacking the three layers together from the centre outwards. The lines of tacking need to be no more than 3 or 4in (7.5–10cm) apart. It helps to use a small spoon in your free hand to encourage the needle to resurface.

Alternatively, use a traditional rectangular frame. For a detailed description of this method see *The Complete Book of Quiltmaking* or *Quilts* for photographs of traditional quilters setting work in a frame (see Bibliography, page 118).

MARKING YOUR QUILT

Begin by marking the centre of each side of the quilt. Use tailor's chalk to mark a line across these points to find the centre. Then mark out the different areas of the design: the centre panel with central medallion, one or more borders and corner squares.

It is best to do the rest of the marking as you work, using templates for specific motifs or marking infills such as diamond lattice with a ruler and chalk, or quilter's masking tape.

You may wish to develop your own unique combination of designs as the old Welsh quilters used to do, from the examples of motifs, borders and centres given on pages 104–112.

HAND QUILTING

If you are new to quilting, refer to one of the specialist books, for example *Perfecting the Quilting Stitch* in the Bibliography, page 118.

Hand quilting tips

• Use a good-quality quilting thread and short 'betweens' needles. You will also need a thimble.

• The needle should be as near vertical as possible when it passes through the quilt sandwich so that the stitches on the front and back of the quilt are the same size, and the distance between stitches should be the same size as each stitch (see photographs, right).

• Getting several stitches on the needle at once will help to keep lines straight. However, when sewing circles or spirals it is better to take single stitches.

• Evenness of stitching is more important than size, though the stitches should be small. There should be a very slight tension on the quilting thread so that the wadding (batting) is compressed slightly and the stitches lie in a small dip, but the work must not be gathered up.

• Start and finish each length of thread unobtrusively with a knot and a backstitch before pulling the remaining thread between the layers. If you are sewing a lot of short lines or small motifs, it is possible to travel through the wadding (batting) of the quilt from one to another without finishing off.

• Use only about 18in (45cm) of thread in the needle at a time to avoid wear on the thread. Waxing the thread can help but will not prevent fraying entirely. If you are sewing around a large circle or square, you can use double the normal length by pulling only half the thread through when taking the first stitch. Sew around half the shape with this thread and finish off. Then re-thread your needle with the other free end and complete the shape. This technique can also be used for long lines of straight quilting, turning your work in the hoop or sewing from the other side of a traditional rectangular frame.

Left: Detail of hand quilting on the reverse of the Brecon Star Quilt, pages 58–63.

i

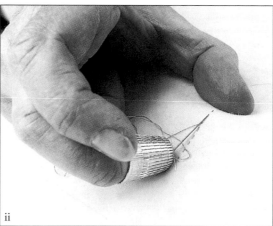

ii

Above: Position of hands when quilting
(i) Use the top of the thimble to push the needle vertically down through the quilt.
(ii) The needle is 'rocked' back by pressing down on the end to bring the tip back to the surface. The index finger underneath 'feels' for the tip of the needle.

MACHINE QUILTING

Machine quilting traditional Welsh designs is not as difficult as it might seem at first. If you are new to free machine quilting, consult a specialist book such as *Quilting from Start to Finish* or *Heirloom Machine Quilting* (see Bibliography, page 118). Many traditional patterns are easily adapted for continuous sewing – practise and have fun!

Machine quilting tips

- Prepare the quilt sandwich by pinning with safety pins at 3–4in (7.5–10cm) intervals, working from the centre out as for hand quilting (see left). This works better than tacking (basting) by hand as the tacking thread tends to snag on the presser foot and/or the machine bed, but safety pins can be removed easily as the foot approaches them.

- Use a dual-feed walking foot, a 'jeans' needle and cotton thread in the bobbin.

- Choose a good-quality 'invisible' monofilament thread and stabilize the quilt by first sewing 'in the ditch' around the central medallion and the borders.

- Mark out your chosen designs with a chalk wheel or watercolour pencil and continue quilting with the 'invisible' thread or one of the many decorative quilting threads available. Use the dual-feed foot if quilting straight lines but drop the feed dogs and use an embroidery or darning foot if you want to sew curved motifs.

- To help you grip the quilt while moving it under the needle, use rubber finger-stalls or a pair of 'quilting' gloves with rubber gripper dots along the fingers and palm. Remember to keep your arms and shoulders as relaxed as possible and to take frequent breaks to avoid getting repetitive strain injuries.

LABELLING YOUR QUILT

Always make sure your quilt has a label showing at least your name and the date, and any other information you think would interest future generations – remember how frustrating it is looking at anonymous quilts from the past and trying to guess their history.

HAND APPLIQUE

This technique is needed for both the Cariad Quilt projects (pages 40–43 and 64–67).

1 When applying motifs to the quilt top by hand, first trace the required template on to freezer paper and cut out.
2 Iron the freezer paper shiny side down on to the reverse of the fabric. Cut out, adding a seam allowance of ¼in (6mm).
3 Fold the seam allowance over the edges of the freezer paper on the straight edges and press, using some spray starch.
4 Snip very carefully into the seam allowance and run a gathering thread, in the seam allowance only, around the outside of the shape.

Pull up the thread so that the fabric fits the template smoothly and press again.
5 While the fabric is still warm, carefully remove the freezer paper with a large quilting pin. Small motifs should hold their shape long enough for you to sew them to the background.
6 Position the motif right side up in the middle of the centre square. Tape in place and sew to the background with small slipstitches about ⅛in (3mm) apart, using thread to match the heart fabric.

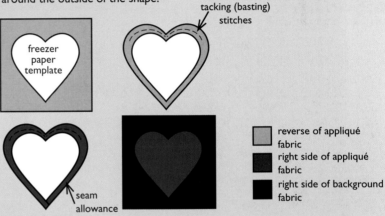

freezer paper template

tacking (basting) stitches

seam allowance

reverse of appliqué fabric

right side of appliqué fabric

right side of background fabric

BUTTED EDGES

Traditional Welsh quilts are finished off with a 'butted', not bound, edge.

1 Cut the surplus backing and wadding (batting) to fit the top.
2 Separate the edges of the top and backing fabrics, and trim the wadding (batting) back a further ⅜in (9mm), taking care not to nick the fabrics.
3 Turn the edges of the top and backing fabrics in and under ¼in (6mm). Quilt as close to the edge as possible. At each corner, fold the seam allowances of the back and front of the quilt in opposite directions and overlap them.
4 Quilt a second line ¼–⅜in (6–9mm) in from this.

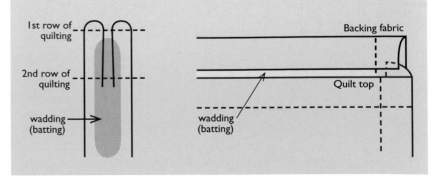

1st row of quilting

2nd row of quilting

wadding (batting)

Backing fabric

Quilt top

wadding (batting)

Places to See Welsh Quilts

It is recommended that you make contact prior to a visit as not all quilts are on permanent display.

Wales

Museum of Welsh Life
St Fagans Castle, Cardiff CF5 6XB
Tel. 029 2057 3500
www.nmgw.ac.uk

The Quilt Association
Minerva Arts Centre, Llanidloes, Powys
Tel. 01686 413467/412278
www.quilt.org.uk

Jen Jones Welsh Quilts
Pontbrenddu, Llanybydder, Ceredigion SA40 9UJ
Tel. 01570 480610
www.jen-jones.com

Carmarthen County Museum
Abergwili, Carmarthenshire SA31 2JG
Tel. 01267 228696
www.carmarthenshire.gov.uk

Ceredigion Museum
Terrace Road, Aberystwyth, Ceredigion SY23 2AQ
Tel. 01970 633088
www.museum.ceredigion.gov.uk

Brecknock Museum and Art Gallery
Captain's Walk, Brecon, Powys LD37 7DW
Tel. 01874 624121
www.powysmuseums.powys.gov.uk

The Cynon Valley Museum and Gallery
Depot Road, Aberdare, Mid Glamorgan CF44 8DL
Tel. 01685 886729

National Woollen Museum
Dre-fach Felindre, Llandysul, Carmarthenshire
SA44 5UP
Tel. 01559 370929
www.nmgw.ac.uk

Outside Wales

The Quilters' Guild of the British Isles,
Room 190, Dean Clough, Halifax, West Yorkshire,
England HX3 5AX
Tel. 01422 347669
www.quiltersguild.org.uk

Bibliography

Quilt history

Colby, Averil (1972) *Quilting* Batsford, London

FitzRandolph, Mavis (1954) *Traditional Quilting* Batsford, London

FitzRandolph, M. and Fletcher, F.M. (1972) *Quilting* The Dryad Press, Leicester

Hake, Elizabeth (1937) *English Quilting Old and New* Batsford, London.

Jones, Jen (1997) *Welsh Quilts* Towy Publishing, Carmarthen

Quilters' Guild, The (1995) *Quilt Treasures* Deirdre MacDonald Books, London

Rae, Janet (1987) *Quilts of the British Isles* Constable, London

Osler, Dorothy (1987) *Traditional British Quilts* Batsford, London

Scott, Beatrice (1935) *The Craft of Quilting* The Dryad Press, Leicester

Stevens, Christine (1993) *Quilts* Gomer Press (in association with the National Museum of Wales), Wales

Welsh history

Morgan, Prys and Thomas, David (1984) *Wales: The Shaping of a Nation* David & Charles, Newton Abbot

Thomas, David (2003) *Dyddiaduron Emiah a Mari Jones, Bancyffynnon (Diaries of Emiah and Mari Jones of Bancyffynnon)* David Thomas, Llanelli

Patchwork and quilting techniques

Beyer, Jinny (2004) *Quiltmaking by Hand* Breckling Press, Illinois

Chainey, Barbara (1993) *The Essential Quilter* David & Charles, Newton Abbot

Cory, Pepper (1999) *Mastering Quilt Marking* C&T Publishing Inc., California

Doak, Carol (1997) *Your First Quilt Book (or should be!)* That Patchwork Place, Washington

Guerrier, Katharine (2004) *Quilting from Start to Finish* David & Charles, Newton Abbot

Hargrave, Harriet (1990) *Heirloom Machine Quilting* C&T Publishing Inc., California

Johnson-Sebro, Nancy (1990) *Measure the Possibilities with Omnigrid* C&T Publishing Inc., California

Morris, Patricia J. (2001) *Perfecting the Quilting Stitch* American Quilters Society, USA

Walker, Michele (1989) *The Complete Book of Quiltmaking* Random House, London

Walker, Michele (1990) *The Passionate Quilter* Ebury Press, London

Acknowledgments

We are grateful for the great support and co-operation we have received from museums, collectors, families of the quilt makers and especially for the enduring patience of our friends and family.

We are particularly indebted to Jen Jones and her husband Roger Clive-Powell, who did much of the photography, together with Janet Bridge and Hazel Newman, for their valuable help, advice, generosity in lending their quilts and delightful visits to their home and gallery. Jen, an American, came to Wales and recognized that Welsh woollen quilts were very special and it is through her collecting that so many have been saved from extinction. A new museum to house this famous collection is now being built.

Others too have given us tremendous help. Doreen Gough, the Director of the Quilt Association not only helped us select quilts from their collection but also drove many miles in mid-winter to deliver them for photography. Christine Stevens, the keeper of the quilts at The Museum of Welsh Life, helped us immensely, drawing on her expert knowledge of the subject. Ron Simpson, a Canadian, who like Jen recognized the worth of Welsh quilts and amassed a fine collection, generously shared them with us. The Quilters' Guild of the British Isles allowed us to include and base a project on one of the quilts in their collection. Robert and Ardis James also gave permission for us to use one of their quilts as the basis of a project; this quilt is part of their collection now housed at The International Centre for the Quilt at the University of Nebraska. Thanks too to Dorothy Osler for sharing with us her ongoing research into the Amish/Welsh connection.

Among the other museum curators who have allowed us to include quilts are Belinda Bajai at Cynon Valley Museum, David Moore and his wonderful staff at Brecknock Museum and Michael Freeman and Gwellian Ashley at Ceredigion Museum. We are most grateful to them all.

We would also like to thank friends who have allowed us to include their own family quilts and who have provided us with much relevant information. They include Rosemary and John Evans; Sue Rayfield and Jim Jones; the family of Katy Lewis; Eluned Norton; Norah Howells; Marilyn Rees; Ann Nowell, quilt gatherer extraordinaire, and all at Bedwas; Megan Davies of Tredomen; Sue Warren; David Thomas and Yvonne Scott; Ann Lace and Winifred Jones; Elaine Williams and her cousin Connie from Cwmbach, Aberdare; Janet Harry; Mike Chugg; Ruth Stannard.

Thanks are also due to Havard & Havard of 59 Eastgate, Cowbridge, South Glamorgan for providing the antiques used in the photographs. Help with materials and equipment was given by Creative Grids; Busy Bees, Tredegar Park, Newport; and Cardiff Quilters; and we are extremely grateful to Lynn Jones for testing the instructions for the rotary-cut projects.

We would like to thank everyone at David & Charles for having faith in the book, particularly Vivienne Wells who commissioned it and Ali Myer and Ame Verso who were with us from start to finish; also Katherine James who helped to get it together. Finally we would like to thank all the photographers Kim Sayer, Roger Clive-Powell, Karl Adamson and Simon Whitmore for their help in trying to capture the beauty of the quilts on film, which is not an easy task!

Index